THE STRUGGLE FOR BLACK HISTORY

Foundations for a Critical Black Pedagogy in Education

Abul Pitre
Ruth Ray
Esrom Pitre

University Press of America,® Inc.
Lanham · Boulder · New York · Toronto · Plymouth, UK

Copyright © 2008 by
University Press of America,® Inc.
4501 Forbes Boulevard
Suite 200
Lanham, Maryland 20706
UPA Acquisitions Department (301) 459-3366

Estover Road
Plymouth PL6 7PY
United Kingdom

Library of Congress Control Number: 2007930032
ISBN-13: 978-0-7618-3836-4 (paperback : alk. paper)
ISBN-10: 0-7618-3836-8 (paperback : alk. paper)

⊖™ The paper used in this publication meets the minimum
requirements of American National Standard for Information
Sciences—Permanence of Paper for Printed Library Materials,
ANSI Z39.48—1984

Dedication

This book is in memory of those who struggled to make schools in St. Landry Parish just and equitable for African American children. To Luther Hill, Vernon White, and Willie Pitre: we will never forget your sacrifices.

Table of Contents

Foreword

The multicultural education concept has gone through many metamorphoses within the last four decades. Initially the major thrust was focused on awareness, helping educators to recognize and understand the importance of embracing individual differences and accepting and appreciating the uniqueness of each human being. In the late '60s the National Council for Accreditation of Teacher Education (NCATE) required colleges of education to respond to a standard focused on diversity in order to attain NCATE accreditation for their teacher education programs. Universities in several states decided to withdraw their applications from NCATE for accreditation as part of their resistance to addressing multicultural education issues. Unfortunately with that mentality the multi-cultural education thrust was stifled.

Multicultural education concepts will not prosper in America until we are courageous enough to address the real issue that has caused the problems for 400 years and that problem is racism. Individuals across this country who attempt to address this problem are criticized and viewed as trouble makers in instigating racial unrest. Few people in leadership want to acknowledge the real essence of racism which is about power and control. It is also a form of mental illness. It hurts people of all races. One, it puts a lot of pressure on Caucasian students indicating to them that they are superior intellectually and are expected to do better academically. Based on that premise for many years those students were allowed an educational experience that was better than the education experience provided for students of color. The buildings were very well maintained, the teachers were paid a higher salary, the financial allocation for those schools were often triple the allocation provided for predominately black schools. In spite of the high degree of oppression and discrimination, many black students blossomed and became world leaders and changed the course of world history. However, that false sense of superiority has caused many young Caucasian students to have severe emotional, mental and socialization problems because psychologically they recognized they had weaknesses and strengths just like other human beings and even with all of the opportunities they still found themselves only being human. Historically every society has a group of people who seem to have a need to look down on another group to feel of worth and in this country until we get intellectually astute, leaders who are visionary, strong and confident enough in themselves to make healing racism a national issue it will not be resolved.

Thus, *The Struggle for Black History* is a dynamic book that addresses many critical issues that if critically analyzed would strengthen the fiber of teaching and learning in this country so that all students may develop to their fullest potential and make a meaningful contribution to this society.

Rose Duhon-Sells, Ph.D.
Vice Chancellor for Academic Affairs
Southern University at New Orleans
National Association of Multicultural
Education Founder

Preface

As we enter the seventh year of the new millennium, the struggle for Black history remains a major issue in the education of American youth. Some of the historical and contemporary issues around the implementation of Black history include: What counts as knowledge? Whose knowledge will prevail in the curriculum? Many of these same issues existed when Black history was formally named in 1926 by Carter G. Woodson. Woodson, in his exegesis of Black education, espoused that the education of African Americans was in many cases *mis-education*: "for the Negro's mind has been all but perfectly enslaved in that he has been trained to think what is desired of him" (p. 24). This mis-education played a primary role in convincing African Americans of their supposedly inferior status by teaching a Euro-centered history that reinforced White supremacy and Black inferiority. The Black movement from the 1930s to the 1960s created new ideas about the need for Black history.

Elijah Muhammad played a most significant role in reinforcing the need for Black history by asking, "Who is the original man?" This question forced scholars to reexamine the historical greatness of African Americans. Muhammad further argued that the most essential knowledge needed by African Americans included the knowledge of self and God. Malcolm X, a student of Elijah Muhammad and a leading spokesman, as well as other ministers of Elijah Muhammad, awakened and re-awakened the need for Black history. Of course, this movement was seen as a threat to the ruling class, and it created a wave of controversy evidenced by the Black movement in the 1960s, which disrupted business as usual and forced the educational institutions of America to change course. The result was the implementation of Black studies and Black student unions on college campuses. The movement also served as a springboard for multicultural education, which is concerned with creating educational equality. However, the push for Black studies, while becoming institutionalized on university campuses, remains largely ignored in K-12 settings. This has resulted in a continued cycle of mis-education that is transferred to the larger society.

Today, schools have moved even further away from Woodson's, Garvey's, and Muhammad's ideas about Black history. In fact, most schools that serve African American students are primarily concerned with meeting standardized testing requirements; thus, the whole purpose of education is lost. It is not unusual for a child to attend school from K-12 and know very little about the accomplishments of Black people to the world. This lack of historical knowledge has served the purpose of maintaining White supremacy and Black inferiority, and has resulted in Black students devaluing self. Ogbu (1995) reinforces this point when he notes that being smart is viewed by some African American students as "acting White." The deprivation of historical knowledge about Black accomplishment is directly connected to ideology and power.

Watkins (2001) points out that the "White architects" of Black education never intended for African Americans to have an education that would truly free them. These architects understood the importance of ideology, power, and the influence of studying one's history. The study of history serves as the springboard for action. To keep a people inactive, you must deprive them of their history. Farrakhan brilliantly elucidates the importance of history:

> When you rob from a man his history and make him think he's nothing: Jesus said, "As a man thinketh in his heart so is he." History is our guide and without history we are lost. . . . The Honorable Elijah Muhammad says that history develops the springs and motives of human actions which display itself most powerfully on the destiny of man. When we read the autobiography of great men and women, their autobiography develops the springs and motives for human action, because when you read about great men and women, there is something in their lives which inspires things in your life because their life shows us the realm of possibility. But when you strip a people of how to look for the history of others to develop the motives of their own actions to spring them into activity, you have deprived them of that motivating, stimulating force, and so the people are dead, and the dead know not anything, and so their condition remains the same from year to year. (Eure & Jerome, 1989, pp. 52-55)

The stimulating force of history has been hidden from African American students. Recently in Lafayette, Louisiana, a controversy erupted over the implementation of Black history being taught in the public schools. The school board voted 7-2 against the implementation of Black history in the schools. The two proponents of Black history were African American board members who voted for its implementation, while the seven White board members voted against it. This brings to light two important issues that we must examine regarding Black education: 1) who controls the system of education? and 2) what is the inspirational value of Black history?

Woodson (1999) explains the first issue with his argument that education is outside of the control of Black people. Woodson suggests that the education of Black people is entirely in the hands of those who once enslaved them and now oppress them. Secondly, Woodson points out education must "inspire people to live more abundantly, to learn to begin life as they find it and make it better" (p.29). The educational system, in America has been a main handicap in giving African Americans the opportunity to truly become free. The omission of a critical and truthful examination of Black history by the shapers of education has continued the process of mis-education for the masses of American youth. When Black history is properly implemented, it has the potential to transform individuals, schools, and society.

The Struggle for Black History: Foundations for a Critical Black Pedagogy in Education demonstrates what can happen when students are taught critical Black history. The students in this book, like some African American students across this nation, were afflicted by gang violence, drugs, family issues, and economic issues, had low self-esteem, low test scores, no interest in school, and were disruptive and confused with a number of other issues. However, through critical Black history, these students were able to transform their lives and their school. In spite of the positive impact of this Black history program and Black studies curriculum at this school, the struggle for Black history was illuminated by those who wish to maintain schools where African Americans should be convinced of their so-called inferiority. The struggle for Black history continues!

Abul Pitre
Edinboro, PA
February 2007

Acknowledgments

We would like to acknowledge Clifton Lemelle, Marion White, Joshua Pitre, Father McKnight, Donald Pitre, and others who have inspired the struggle for Black history. This work would never have come into existence were it not for Catherine Pierre. Thanks, Ms. Pierre for providing us with newspaper clippings and other documents necessary to make this research project a reality. To all of you who protested the inequities of African American children in St. Landry parish, we thank you. A special thanks to the following people: Pastor Dale Fontenot, Reverend and Sister Johnson, Rose Sam, The Doucet's, Ms. Stoot, The Tezeno's, and others—Thanks! A special thanks to graduate students, Kobie Griffin and Marica Harris. Dr. James Banning your inspiration and guidance of this work shall never be forgotten. Most importantly we thank God for his divine intervention in our affairs.

Chapter 1

Diversity, Protest, and Racism in Education

Public school systems throughout America have been faced with the problem of implementing curricula that reflect a pluralistic society, particularly curricula regarding the African American experience (Banks, 2002; Wilhelm, 1994). This problem has often led to student protest in which students have demanded the implementation of courses that reflect a more diverse society (Rhoads, 1998a; "Proposal to scuttle Afrocentric curricula," 1997). Administrators and teachers have hypothesized ways to promote a more multicultural-centered curriculum; however, in many school systems, the idea of a multicultural curriculum has not yet become a reality.

Schools in Wisconsin, California, and Louisiana have witnessed student protest as a result of Black History activities. In Milwaukee, a school board member's effort to remove Afrocentric curricula from the schools resulted in an emotional protest by hundreds of parents and raised questions about what is being taught in multicultural programs ("Proposal to scuttle Afrocentric curricula," 1997). In Los Angeles, two racial flare-ups demonstrated the challenges faced by many school districts. In February 1999, a White principal at a mostly Hispanic elementary school was beaten up outside of the school by two men who told him, "We don't want you here anymore, Principal." In another incident, Inglewood High School dropped both Black History Month and Cinco de Mayo for fear of the violence and student walkouts that have occurred in the past. Added to the problem at Inglewood was that after dropping these programs, the school was forced to close for one day in May because of a riot that required dozens of police to be called in ("L. A. schools battle," 1999).

A protest situation in Louisiana made the headlines for several weeks, with the controversy lasting well over one year. The controversy began when a few White teachers walked out of a Black History Program, prompting African American students, parents, and teachers to become upset. Immediately following the Black History Program, a White teacher was believed to have phoned the school board to inform them that there would be trouble at the school as a result of the Black History Program. The next day the school was surrounded with school board personnel, sheriff deputies, and newspaper reporters. The headline of the newspaper read, "A Contingent of School Board administrators and a Cadre of Deputies, including the chief deputy with the Sheriff's Office were patrolling the halls" ("Controversy at High School," 1994).

The Black students complained that during the Black History Month Program a year earlier, just before the speaker arrived, all the White students checked out of school ("Controversy," 1994). One month after the Black History Program in 1994, one of the teachers who walked out of the program had a confrontation with a student. The local newspaper printed on its front page "Teacher Attacked by Student." In the article, the teacher claimed that ever since the speech at the Black History Program, he had felt animosity from Black parents and students at the school ("Teacher Attacked," 1994). As a result of these events, the Black parents demanded that the teachers who walked out of the program be removed from the school. A parent leader of a newly formed organization called Concerned Parents stated, "We are asking the two teachers to resign because they are racist. It has happened before and it just got bad after the Black History Program" ("School Troubles," 1994).

The President of the local National Association for the Advancement of Colored People (NAACP) expressed his feelings about the situation by saying,

> The system is racist for allowing those types of things to happen. . . . We met with the superintendent last year about White teachers leading White students out of those programs. We approached the superintendent a week prior to the assembly and asked that a policy be established. ("Parents want to oust principal, 2 teachers" 1994)

Other problems with the implementation of Black History curricula can be seen in studies conducted by Alexander (1982) and Wilhelm (1994). In a study of 36 elementary public school principals in Chesapeake and Maryland public school systems, Alexander reported that even though February was designated as Black History Month, this had "negligible impact on actual observances in the schools." Wilhelm studied 48 elementary schools in the Dallas Fort Worth area, and he reported that many of the schools had no policy regarding the implementation of Black History Month. Wilhelm stated, "The large percentage of schools with no planned observances suggested that this kind of laissez-faire policy may be common place in most districts" (p. 220).

The discovery that most school districts have no policy with regards to Black History Month is consistent with Alexander's findings, as he stated, ". . . no signs of leadership were offered at the central administration level to actually provide programmatic leadership [regarding Black History Month] to the schools" (Alexander, 1982, p. 6). As Wilhelm (1994) describes it, "most public school curricula related to Black History and culture is antiseptic and lacking in analysis of the Black experience in a meaningful and real life manner" (p. 217). While administrators and teachers are cognizant of this problem, solutions have been slow in coming. This book explores student activists' experiences regarding the controversy and student protest surrounding a Black History Program at their school.

The problem of implementing a multicultural curriculum is one that is not going away. Today, the current curriculum is being challenged to become more multicultural (Banks, 2002). Challenges are being put forward by African Americans, Asian Americans, and Latinos "for full structural inclusion and a reformulation of the canon used to select content for the school, college, and university curriculum" (p. 25). Furthermore, coalitions are being formed with White students who wish to see a more inclusive curriculum (Banks, 2002).

Issues around the implementation of Black History and multicultural curricula have caused a new student movement that was the primary cause of student activism in the 1990s (Rhoads, 1998b). Rhoads "found multiculturalism to be the number one cause of student unrest in the 1990s" (p. 24). Add to this the fact that it is projected that by the year 2020, students of color will make up 46 percent of the nation's school-age youth (Pallas, Natriello, & McDill, 1989).

Under the umbrella of multicultural education curriculum reform is the push for Black History, which is sometimes synonymously used with Afrocentric History (Banks, 2002). African American students, parents, and community groups are leading the push for curriculum that reflects the experience of Africans and African Americans (Chemelynski, 1990; Lee, 1992). This challenge, according to Banks (2002), "is likely to continue, will be fierce and will at times become ugly and pernicious. It will take diverse forms, expressions, and shapes" (p. 27).

In order to alleviate such problems from becoming overwhelming we believe it is important to study this controversy and protest with regard to the implementation of Black History. More importantly, this study is needed to ascertain what the experience is like for individuals involved. This could go a long way in helping those for and against the implementation of Black History to reach some common ground. A major problem with the implementation of Black History lies in the lack of studies about the experiences of proponents and opponents of this issue.

The purpose of this study was to examine the experiences of student leaders in order to ascertain how their experiences of the Black History Program and student protest were viewed at the time of the controversy and the effect of this phenomenon on their personal lives. Findings from this study can enhance the knowledge base of school districts and administrators planning to implement Black History into the curriculum. Furthermore, these experiences may provide an additional opportunity for school administrators to look at the impact of Black History on the attitudes of students. Lastly, findings from this study demonstrate the impact of student activism on the development of leadership characteristics of students.

The primary goal of this study, therefore, was to determine how a Black History Program and student protest impacted student attitudes about school. In addition, the study examined how student worldviews have been shaped as result of this experience. This study, unlike others that have focused on college student protest, focused on a high school student protest and the student activist experiences. The study highlights the experience of student leaders who were at odds with lead administrators and school board members regarding issues which surrounded a Black History Program. What makes this study unique is that it captures the high school student leader experiences about activities associated with this phenomenon.

The research on student activism suggested the need for a phenomenological study to examine the narrative experience of student activists. We modified Seidman's (1998) approach, which uses in-depth phenomenological interviews to ascertain the narrative experience of student activists. This approach has three levels of questioning: 1) Background information about the participants, 2) investigating how individuals recall events associated with the phenomenon in relationship to their personal thoughts and actions, and 3) exploring the meaning and impact of the phenomenon on participants. The three levels of questioning were arranged in the following format:

1) Students' ages and a description of their family background with regards to socio-economic status and education.

2) What was the essence of the Black History Program and Student Protest?
   a) How do participants remember events associated with the Black History Program and Student Protest?
   b) What motivated students to engage in protest?
   c) What were the objectives of the student protest?
   d) How far were students willing to go to have their demands met?

e) How did students perceive faculty and staff response to student activism and student protest?

3) Has this phenomena impacted the students' perspective of the world?

Research Cautions

The reader should be cautioned that this study includes only student leaders within the same Louisiana school district. It should also be noted that the data was limited to the experiences of student leaders. As a result, the accuracy of the findings is dependent upon the degree of objectivity and honesty of the individual students. Furthermore, the time period between the occurrence of the events and the interview of the participants could affect the students' recollection of events. Finally, the findings of this study cannot entirely be generalized to other student protest movements in different schools.

Chapter 2

Education for Freedom

One of the major issues in education that must be examined is the political nature of education. On the surface, education appears to most people as something that is apolitical, but in reality, politics is at the core of education. According to Darder (2002) Freire notes, "The politics of education is part and parcel of the very nature of education. . . . It does not matter where or when it has taken place, whether it is more or less complex, education has always been a political act" (pp. 126-127) Darder expounds on Freire's analysis that schools perform the function of politicizing and socializing children to their roles in the society: "Thus education must be understood as a politicizing (or depoliticizing) institutional process that conditions students to subscribe to the dominant ideological norms and political assumptions of the prevailing social order" (p. 56). From its inception, teaching has been about sorting and selecting individuals to fit the demands of a capitalist society. In her study, Anyon (1981) outlined how schools reproduce the class issues that exist in the larger society. Anyon's study described four types of schools that were ranked according to the income of the students' parents. Those schools were labeled working class schools, middle class schools, affluent schools, and executive elite schools. In each of these schools, the hidden curriculum prepared the students to fit a particular function in the society, which in effect reproduced what existed in the larger society. The study has profound implications, as 85 percent of the students in this study were White. This in itself should be cause for great concern for the African American student. If schools perform this reproducing act on White students, what might this suggest for African American students who historically were denied the right to proper education? Woodson elaborates on the function of education for African Americans as primarily serving the purpose of mis-educating African Americans.

A significant part of African American history has involved a process of education that was concerned with making them fit into a racist and capitalist society. Woodson prophetically saw the education of African Americans as tool that primarily benefited those in dominant positions. In the present state of affairs, African Americans are in the same relative position as their ancestors who first set foot on American shores to be made slaves. One could argue that African Americans have progressed tremendously since the Emancipation Proclamation. Some would argue the fact that African Americans hold high political positions, have been educated in some of the finest universities, and have attained prominent status in almost every endeavor of American life. However, if one were to look more deeply, they would find that African Americans have very little control in making major educational decisions. The education of African American students is ultimately controlled by those in dominant positions. Woodson eloquently noted that the few Negroes who serve on educational boards do not have the power to really change the educational systems that impact African American children. In those cases where African Americans make up the majority in the decision-making process, they are not equipped with authority or understanding at the root of educational problems facing African Americans. This is best seen in many of the major urban areas where some school leaders have been reduced to technicians, making administrators merely managers of oppressive schools as opposed to school leaders who have a vision for transformation. This dumbing down of school leaders and the need to meet the *No Child Left Behind* mandates have rendered the education of the African American student necrophilic, thus keeping the African mind in a state of death. Freire (2000) makes a similar observation when he states that "oppression—overwhelming control—is necrophilic; it is nourished by love of death, not life" (p. 77).

A major dilemma in understanding how to educate African Americans is the fact that most people do not understand or want to acknowledge that the slave-making process was educational. To understand this process, we need look no further than Edwin R. Embree's *Brown Americans*, where Embree notes the words of Henry Berry speaking to house of Virginia delegates in 1832:

> We have as far as possible, closed every avenue by which light may enter the slave mind. If we could extinguish the capacity to see the light, our work would be complete; they would then be on a level with the beast of the field and we should be safe. I am not certain that we would not do it, if we could find out the process and that on the plea of necessity. (Muhammad, 1965, pp. 185-186)

In other writings that have been attributed to someone called Willie Lynch, the process of making and controlling a slave involves a particular methodology:

> I have a foolproof method of controlling your Black slaves. I guarantee every one of you that if installed correctly, it will control the slaves for at least 300 hundred years. My method is simple. Any member of your family or your over-

seer can use it. I have outlined a number of differences among the slaves, and I take these differences and make them bigger. I use fear, distrust and envy for control purposes. (Hassan-El, 1999)

Lynch summarized the education process in the following words, "Hence both the horse and the nigger must be broken that is break them from one form of mental life to another—keep the body and take the mind" (Hassan-El, 1999, p. 14). This process of making a slave has not been carefully diagnosed by educators and is a major problem in truly understanding how to educate African Americans for freedom. Clarke (1919) brilliantly explains this dilemma when he says that Africans were not brought to the new world to be educated but instead to be a part of the labor supply. The education of African Americans both historically and contemporarily is in need of two major components: the knowledge of self and a reexamination of Black critical pedagogist ideas about Black education.

The education of African Americans has been primarily concerned with making them better servants in a capitalist system that serves the interests of those in dominant positions. In order to reverse the mis-education that has been taking place, African American students must first be given knowledge of self. This knowledge of self will lay the base for re-awakening the Black mind. Karenga (2002) notes that of all the immigrants that have come to America, the African American has been completely stripped of a true knowledge of self. This stripping of knowledge has resulted in amnesia. The African American, if asked his origin, name, language, or culture, is unable to reply, thus rendering him an amnesia victim. To reverse this amnesia, African Americans need a history of themselves that dates back beyond their history in America. Too often, the accomplishments of African Americans are confined to Black accomplishments in White America. However, the knowledge of self is not simply about examining great African queens, kings, scientists, mathematicians, educators, etc., but it is ultimately looking back at the relationship between the African American and God. Naim Akbar (1998), in his book *Know Thy Self*, notes the following role of education: "The major premise of effective education must be 'self–knowledge.' In order to achieve the goals of identity and empowerment that we have described above, the educational process must be one that educes the awareness of who we are" (p. 17). The process of educing this awareness is where the dilemma may lie. According to Akbar, "This aspect of the education in self-knowledge creates a serious conflict for the European American educational process. The conflict is a result of the rigid separation between church and state which has been established in their concept of education" (p. 50). Another problem is that in order to educe an awareness of self African Americans must travel back in time to uncover who they were before their arrival to America. In most schools, any discussion that will lead to a true understanding of self will create a firestorm from a wide array of people. However, to properly educate the African American student, one must consider what Akbar (1998) refers to as "transmitting acquired immunities":

We know now that people who have survived exposure to certain diseases are able to transmit immunity to those diseases through their genes, the mother's milk while being breast-fed. We appreciate that our ability to survive hundreds of diseases that decimated populations before us is a consequence of this immunity that has been transmitted to us through the blood of our parents. Again, this serves an analogy for another of the functions of education. In addition to the bringing forth of identity and transmitting the legacy of competence, education must also transmit many of the acquired immunities that have been learned by earlier generations and their exposure to a variety of intellectual and social diseases. (p. 9)

In understanding the idea of developing knowledge of self, one must not mistake this to mean simply an individual identity but one that is tied to a holistic identity that transcends the individual, eventually leading to knowledge of self and others. The idea of self is not a new concept in education; Pinar (2004) mentions the fact that Dewey "insisted that educational experience provided a bridge between 'self' and 'society,' between self-realization and democratization" (p. 17). The threat to White dominance can be seen in the idea of knowledge of self. A true understanding of self in relationship to others would help African Americans see what White America has made them. To understand the relationship between self and others is the political act of mis-education that White America continues to enforce upon African Americans. This has contributed to some of the major misunderstandings by the masses of people about the need for knowledge of self.

Karenga (2002), one of the leading proponents of Black studies, has defined what is called *Kawaida theory* as way of exploring the knowledge of self. He describes it as "a theory of cultural and social change which has as one of its main propositions, the contention that the solution to the problems of Black life demand critiques and corrections in seven basic areas of culture" (p. 26). Those seven areas are the major components of Black Studies (history, religion, economics, sociology, politics, creative production, and psychology). Kawaida theory is the knowledge of an individual's, past, present, and future possibilities. To understand the past, present, and future possibilities of oneself enables one to produce based on past accomplishments and current circumstances. The major premise of Kawaida is "know thyself."

Kawaida theory is an essential component for African Americans in the process of developing a true self-concept. Karenga notes "a people whose achievements are minor or whose knowledge of its history and the possibilities it suggests is deficient, develops a self consciousness of similar characteristics" (p. 70).

In helping us to understand why knowledge of self has not been implemented in schools, Freire (2000) gives us a plethora of ideas that could enhance our understanding of what typically happens in school and beyond. Freire notes that one of the major issues confronting schools is the technical nature in which they operate. According to Freire, students are simply helpless receptacles into which teachers deposit information. This scenario is too often played out in schools that are predominantly African American. In many cases, the schools are filled with White teachers who have no knowledge of the historical reality of their students. Teachers in many schools that serve African Americans in poor school districts

> . . . organize a process which already occurs spontaneously, to fill the students by making deposits of information which he or she considers to constitute true knowledge. . . . Translated into practice, this concept is well suited to the purposes of the oppressors, whose tranquility rests on how well people fit the world the oppressors have created, and how little they question it. (p. 76)

Schooling thus remains a dictate from the ruling class that is supposedly designed to make everyone equal. In believing the myth that schools perform an equalizing act, the uncritical teacher assumes that the African American student, because of their socio-economic status, dress, language, and behavior, has arrived at this point because of their own shortcomings. This often leads to policies that make schools simply modern plantations with some African American students being held hostage for several hours a day. In the controversy around this Black history program, one of the major issues of concern for students was the policies that were designed to keep the students mentally enslaved, negating praxis. This mental enslavement has resulted in the oppressor justifying unjust school policies.

Freire provides profound insight into the thinking of the oppressor consciousness and the oppression that exist in schools:

> If they do not have more, it is because they are incompetent and lazy, and worst of all is their unjustifiable ingratitude toward the generous gestures of the dominant class. Precisely because they are ungrateful and envious, the oppressed are regarded as potential enemies who must be watched. (p. 59)

The impact of this negative situation could possibly contribute to African American students developing apathy or student resistance to oppressive structures. This might also lead to negative self images, as students might come to believe that these oppressive structures are result of their own doing. Freire describes this as self-deprecation,

> Self deprecation is another characteristic of the oppressed, which derives from their internalization of the opinion of the oppressors hold of them. So often they hear they are good for nothing, know nothing and are incapable of learning anything-that they are sick, lazy, and unproductive-that in the end they become convinced of their own unfitness. (p. 63)

In many cases, this has resulted in the violence that occurs within the school and larger community of African Americans.

Educators have often sought to address the issue of violence by simply looking at the African American student and his/her community background.

Freire points out that violence is never initiated by the oppressed, but it is the oppressed who are shaped in violence and will often begin to manifest a dual consciousness. Fanon (1968) notes that "this is the period when the niggers beat each other up." Freire (2000) makes the assertion that in many cases, to be is to be like the oppressor. This often leads to "the destruction of life- their own or that of their oppressed fellows." As you read the chapters of this book, you will find that these words hold true. In not understanding how they are shaped by a historical legacy, some African Americans will tend to take out their frustrations on people who look like them, act like them, and behave like them. For many students, the saying that "a nigger ain't good for nothing" is translated to mean "if I am a nigger, and he is a nigger then ain't nothing wrong with killing a nigger." This attitude is often reflected in the larger community and reinforced in school where students have no voice.

What happens when liberating education mixes with oppressive education? We will not go in-depth here but as you read chapter four we will examine what happens when students begin to discover the oppressor consciousness within themselves.

When students discover the source of their oppression, the possibility of revolution has been enhanced. Freire (2000) notes that "sooner or later, these contradictions may lead formerly passive students to turn against their domestication and the attempt to domesticate reality" (p. 75). In the final analysis, students will begin to engage in a fight for their liberation. As you read the case study, you will find that students who were at one point fighting with each other began to develop a critical consciousness which paved the way for them to fight for their freedom. This newfound praxis was the result of students being involved in their own learning, but more importantly, experiencing problem-posing education, which is liberating. Freire (2000) states,

> Students as they are increasingly posed with problems relating to themselves in the world and with the world, will feel increasingly challenged and obliged to respond to that challenge. . . . Their response to the challenge evokes new challenges, followed by new understandings; and gradually the students come to regard themselves committed. (p. 81.)

This liberating type of thinking is threatening to those who have an oppressor consciousness, because the ultimate aim of education is not to free but enslave. The following statement by Freire summarizes the challenge of education for freedom:

> Education as the practice of freedom-as opposed to education as the practice of domination—denies that man is abstract, isolated, independent, and unattached to the world; it also denies that the world exists as a reality apart from people. Authentic reflection considers neither abstract man nor the world without people, but people in their relations with the world. In these relations consciousness and world are simultaneous: consciousness neither precedes the world nor follows it. (p. 81)

In conclusion, the controversy around Black history has not been limited to K-12 schools but has been an ongoing issue of debate among scholars. In the next chapter, we examine this debate by considering opponents and proponents of Black history.

Chapter 3

The Controversy around Black History

When Carter G. Woodson declared Negro History Week in 1926, a controversy began that would continue into the twenty-first century. Woodson's Negro History Week was a major step in the process of eradicating many of the problems that confront African Americans as a result of the institution of slavery. Some of those problems include lack of meaningful education, self-knowledge, and self-esteem. The idea of Black History has stirred controversy since its inception and continues to be an important issue in the educational arena. Opponents of the idea have argued that its implementation into the curriculum will be dishonest, divisive, and will make children ill-prepared for the work force. Proponents of Black History believe that it will promote cultural diversity, develop self-esteem, and correct many of the myths espoused by the Euro-centric curriculum. Carter G. Woodson was confronted with many of the current arguments that attempted to keep Black History out of the curriculum. It is important to note that the terms *Black History* and *Afrocentricity* are used synonymously. The definition of each term has Africa at the center of shaping ideas and both are interested in people of African descent in America.

Over the years, Negro History Week has evolved into Black History Month, which was signed into law by President Jimmy Carter (Sesay, 1996). Prior to Carter signing Black History Month into law, student protest in the 1960s involved issues with regard to Black Studies. Presently, the controversy around Black History continues to be a problem that confronts American institutions and public education institutions in particular.

Some of the opponents of Afrocentricity believe that such implementation into the current curriculum will "make Europe and the U.S. rogue elephants of the world history" (Bennett, 1992). According to Bennett, Afro-centrists will assert that North American culture is an offshoot of Western European philosophy and that both are offshoots of African culture. In her book *Not Out of Africa: How Afrocentrism Became an Excuse To Teach Myth as History*, Lefkowitz (1996) asserts that "Afrocentric mythologies of the ancient world appear to have been created," and they are simply mythologies rather than history. Teaching fiction is harmful according to Lefkowitz, who stated, "suppose we allow one particular group to rewrite history to its own specification, and suppose that we judge the groups' ultimate aims to be laudable" (1996). Lefkowitz's primary assertion is that Afrocentricity, or Black History, has been contrived by African American scholars in their attempt to rewrite history.

Another argument against the implementation of Black History is that it causes divisiveness and that students will lack basic work skills if they concentrate on this subject. In their book *Changing Multiculturalism*, Kincheloe and Steinberg argue that monoculturalists believe when African Americans learn of the historical injustice perpetrated against them, they will seek vengeance against White people (1997). They further argue that this is senseless and is used to eliminate Black History from being implemented into the curriculum. Kincheloe and Steinberg state:

> Such an argument could gain credence and plausibility only in a society where people of African descent were viewed as naturally violent. . . . Any program or curriculum that induces people of African descent to group themselves in opposition to white policies must be squashed in the name of our mutual safety as white people. (p. 7)

Schlesinger (1991) contends that Afrocentricity is used as a method of therapy for African Americans, and will result in the "corruption of history as history." According to Schlesinger, this will result in "self-pity and self-ghettoization" of African American students. The implementation of Afrocentricity and multiculturalism deviates from the original purpose of the American republic, which is to create a common identity among the people of America (1991).

The idea of a common identity has meant for African Americans the loss of self-identity. This loss of self-identity has resulted in self-hatred, which has made African Americans of very little service to their own community, while yet serving the needs of a Eurocentric value system. Asante (1991) mentions that in most classrooms, the center of perspective is white. This leaves the African American child to feel like a bystander in the classroom (1991). A good example of this is seen in the work of Kozol's (1991) observation of an elementary classroom:

> The children recite the verses with her as she turns the pages of the book. She's not very warm or animated as she does it, but the children are obedient and seem to like the fun of showing that they know the words. The book looks worn and old, as if the teacher's used it many, many years, and it shows no signs of adaptation to the race of children in the school. Mary is white. Old Mother

Hubbard is white. Jack is white. Jill is white. Little Jack Horner is white. Mother Goose is white. Only Mother Hubbard's dog is black. (p. 45)

Asante (1991) does not see Afrocentricity as an equivalent to Euro-centricity. While Afrocentricity focuses on an African-centered perspective, it does not contend that Afrocentricity is the sum total of reality. The Afrocentric theory is seen by its scholars (Nobles, 1986; Hilliard, 1978; Karenga, 2002; Keto, 1990; Richards, 1991) as a method to provide every American child with a curriculum that is not comprised of a mono-ethnic hegemonic perspective. The Afrocentric theory has three main focuses:

1) It questions the imposition of the White supremacist view as universal and/or classical.
2) It demonstrates the indefensibility of racist theories that assault multi-culturalism and pluralism.
3) It projects a humanistic and pluralistic viewpoint by articulating Afro-centricity as a valid, non-hegemonic perspective (Asante, 1991).

Vann and Kunjufu (1993) demonstrate how the current curriculum has a Eurocentric value system. According to the researchers, the discovery of America by Columbus and the celebration of Thanksgiving both demonstrate the Eurocentric point of view and value system. The Afrocentric, multicultural perspective would challenge the notion of the Columbus discovery of America and ask the question: How do Native people view the celebration of Thanksgiving?

Karenga (2002) views the implementation of Black History as a source of self understanding comprised of three major categories: 1) need for identity, 2) need for understanding of the world and society, and 3) need for "the measure of people's humanity."

The institution of slavery has affected the mentality of African Americans to the degree of creating what is called historical amnesia (Karenga, 2002). Black History serves the purpose of helping African Americans understand themselves by looking at the uniqueness and origin of their history in relation to the development of world history. Black History encourages African Americans to embrace their personal identity as opposed to negating themselves.

Secondly, Black History serves the purpose of helping African Americans understand where they fit into the global scheme of society. Karenga also sees history as cyclical, which means that peoples and nations have what is called "tides of history." An understanding of history would help African Americans accept that they will become a productive and free people as the tide of history changes.

Thirdly, Black History debunks the myth that African Americans did not belong to humanity. The study of African and African American history exposes the world to the great contributions that African people made to the world (Karenga, 2002). Perhaps the best statement about the need for Black History is that

> . . . Black History is a contribution to an indispensable part of the rescue and
> reconstruction of Black humanity. For history is the substance and mirror of a
> people's humanity in others eyes as well as in their own eyes. It is then, not
> only what they have done, but also a reflection of who they are, what they can
> do, and equally important what they can become as a result of the past which
> reveals their possibilities. (p. 69)

Bernal (1996), in his reply to Lefkowitz, believes that "history is fictional," which leaves much open to interpretation. Bernal also believes that professors like Lefkowitz have not painstakingly taken the time to research the assertions made by scholars who study Afro-centrism. It is this misinterpretation of the facts about Black History that has caused confusion about the need for Black History.

Proponents of Black History have argued that a multicultural education helps students develop self-esteem as well as an appreciation for cultural diversity (Heard, 1990). Other reasons for promoting Black History are that it will: 1) Increase self-esteem in African Americans, 2) motivate students to learn, and 3) give students alternative attitudes and values. Perhaps the most important aspect of Black History Month is that it introduces the world to the history of African Americans (Young, 1980).

In 1926, Woodson (1999) started Negro History Week as a result of his discontent with the public school's curricula with regards to Black History. Woodson contended that history of African Americans was nonexistent in the textbooks and when African Americans were mentioned, it was in an inferior status. According to Woodson, this caused African American children to develop a sense of inferiority. He stated, "Even schools for Negroes, then, are places where they must be convinced of their inferiority." This inferiority of African Americans was demonstrated in the textbooks and classrooms. In essence, the education of African Americans made them feel inferior: "The thought of inferiority of the Negro is drilled into him in almost every class he enters and every book he studies" (p. 2). Today, African Americans receive very little mention in history books. The true story of African Americans has yet to be told (Loewen, 1995). Woodson was indeed very prophetic with regard to problems that confront African Americans today.

In his book *The Mis-education of the Negro*, Carter G. Woodson described many of the present day scenarios that negate the essence of Black History. He mentioned several of the problems that confront African Americans today in terms of education and the implementation of Black History. One of the major problems is the high incarceration rate of African American males. Woodson clearly describes a possible reason for such: "As another has well said, to handicap a student by teaching him that his black face is a curse and that his struggles to change his condition is the worst sort of lynching. It kills one's aspirations and dooms him to vagabondage and crime" (p. 3). Today, few schools have implemented a curriculum that would meet Woodson's standards for educating

African Americans and as a result, we see the overrepresentation of African Americans in the penal system (Green, 1991).

In the initial stages of implementing a Black History curriculum, Woodson mentioned many of the present-day debates regarding the implementation of Black History. Many African Americans and Whites were in disagreement with Woodson's implementation of Black History Month. Opponents thought that teaching students Black History would cause a problem between the races. They suggested that such topics should not be taught until students were in college (Woodson, 1999). Woodson contended that students are confronted with the race problem every day, so why not expose them to the truth? In the controversy regarding the speaker at this Black History program, a school board member responded that the program "would have been more appropriate for college students rather than high school students" ("School Plans Apology," 1994). The same school board member also responded, "Parents were upset by an outsider coming in and in their opinion, was trying to divide blacks and whites in this community. I [School board member] too, feel that it is unfortunate that outside forces made an attempt to divide the relationship between blacks and whites" ("School Plans Apology," 1994). The debate continues on when to implement Black History and who should be involved. Perhaps the biggest problem facing the implementation of some Black History celebrations is related to what Woodson discussed on those who control the education of African Americans.

African Americans have very little control over the education of themselves or their children. As a result, attempts to implement African American curricula have been met with hostility throughout this nation. In Louisiana, a principal was fired and two African American teachers were transferred as a result of Black History programs ("Personnel," 1995; "Teacher Says Move Racially Motivated," 1999). In Lebeau, Louisiana, a principal was fired and the teacher who organized the school's Black History program was transferred because the program went against the status quo. Organizers of this program invited a speaker from outside of the community and when the principal refused to transfer the teacher, he was fired. A teacher in Baton Rouge, Louisiana publicly stated that he disagreed with the cancellation of the schools' Black History Month program ("Teacher," 1999). As a result of voicing his opinion about the necessity of the Black History program, he was transferred. In Milwaukee, a school board member's request to remove Afrocentric curricula drew emotional protest from parents ("Proposal to Scuttle Afrocentric curricula," 1997). Woodson (1999) saw this as a problem in his day:

> Negroes have no control over their education and have little voice in their other affairs pertaining thereto. In a few cases Negroes have been chosen as members of public boards of education, and some have been appointed members of private boards, but these Negroes are always such a small minority that they do not figure in the final working out of the educational program. The education of

the Negroes, then, the most important thing in the uplift of Negroes, is almost entirely in the hands of those who enslaved them and now segregate them. (p. 22)

Ultimately, the education of African Americans has continued to result in the enslavement of the mind (Young, 1980). With very little control and input in the educational arena, African Americans have continued to fulfill Woodson's words:

When you control a man's thinking you do not have to worry about his actions. You do not have to tell him stand here or go yonder. He will find his proper place and will stay in it. You do not need to send him to the back door. He will go without being told. In fact, if there is no back door he will cut one for his special benefit. His education makes it necessary. (p. xiii)

Despite Woodson's effort to change this reality with his implementation of Negro History Week, many scholars today debate whether the significance of Black History Month has been watered down to mere tokenism. One question some African American scholars have posed about Black History Month is this: Does Black History Month effectively introduce the world to the achievements of African Americans or is it primarily a marketing device for selling books and making African Americans feel good (Franklin, Horne, Cruse, Ballard, & Mitchell, 1998)?

Some African Americans scholars believe that Black History Month is a time for large corporations to make millions of dollars (Franklin et al., 1998). Corporations such as Phillip Morris, Anheuser-Busch, and Coca-Cola have made a token effort to promote Black History in an attempt to increase marketing efforts in the Black community. Franklin and his colleagues suggest that Black History Month has not moved closer to the ideals expressed by its founder. Instead, it has become commercialized and, in their words, "The commercialization of the month that provides hucksters with a longer period in which to sell trinkets and souvenirs, corporations a greater opportunity to display their special brand of civic awareness."

However, Black History Month does have a useful purpose. Some scholars believe that Black History Month provides a number of educational opportunities for people interested in the contributions of African Americans. The following list entails four of their major ideas:

1) A range of opportunity exists nationally as well as internationally for African American history;

2) Black History Month has implications for young African American scholars looking to discover something new or inventive;

3) The celebration of Black History Month is having an impact somewhere in the country; and

4) The story of African Americans must be told.

Despite the fact that Black History Month has become a period for large corporations to make large profits, it also serves a purpose in the education of people about the history of Africans and African Americans. In many of the public school systems, however, Black History Month has merely become a period to pacify African Americans. The essence of Black History Month has become a way to satisfy the need for diversity, but the exposure of historical facts has been limited.

At a Louisiana high school, students walked out of school in protest of the school's Black History program. The students expressed their discontent with the content and format of the Black History program. Students stated that the program was about the accomplishments of African Americans today ("Black History Program sparks protest," 2000) and had merely mentioned African Americans who were involved in athletics, entertainment, and politics. This, according to students, was not about Black History but the accomplishments of many African Americans who didn't make any significant contributions to the African American community. At best, it was tokenism, in which token African Americans were exposed to students. Students expressed their protest with signs reading "Black History or No History." One student expressed the meaning of the protest by saying, "We want to hear about Black History, about how it was in the past."

Black History programs too often include speakers who have a limited knowledge of the history of African Americans or how that history has allowed the speaker to hold his/her present position. Furthermore, speakers who were active in the struggle for the equality of African Americans are very seldom invited to Black History programs. Most of the speakers and the focus of Black History programs have roles that are consistent with the dominant culture (Banks, 2002). As Banks mentions, it is more likely that Sacajawea would be included in the curriculum because she helped Whites conquer Native people, whereas Geronimo would be excluded because he resisted White takeover of Native lands. This scenario is all too often played out during Black History Month. It is fine to mention Dr. King, Andrew Young, and more recently Malcolm X, as long as there is only mention of concepts and ideals that meet the needs of the dominant culture. For example, it is okay to mention Dr. King's dream, but don't mention his opposition to Vietnam (Nieto, 2004) or his meeting with Elijah Muhammad. As Loewen (1995) discusses in his book *Lies My Teacher Told Me*, history books are guilty of biased portrayal of historical events and personalities. This is precisely what Black History has become—a biased display of historical facts, events, and personalities.

The protest by students at this Louisiana High School can best be seen in Banks' model of Multicultural Reform. Banks (2002) describes four levels to the approaches of curriculum reform: contributions approach, additive approach, transformation approach, and social action approach. The contribution approach focuses on heroes, holidays, and cultural events. The additive approach focuses on concepts, themes and perspectives. The transformation approach focuses on the structure of the curriculum that enables students to view concepts, issues, events, and themes from the perspective of diverse ethnic and cultural groups. The social action approach allows students to make decisions on important social issues and take actions to help solve them.

Of these four approaches, the first two are most often used when planning Black History programs. The programs usually coincide with the dominant culture and focus on heroes, concepts, and themes that reflect the bias of the organizers. When the students are given input in the organization of the Black History program, they move to the transformation and social action approaches. The students become capable of viewing concepts, issues, and themes from a multicultural perspective.

A case in point: students organized a Black History program at a southern high school. The students discussed with their advisor their desire to have a program that included a non-traditional guest speaker. In the selection of the speaker, it was agreed upon that the speaker would be of the Islamic faith, which was non-traditional. Added to this was that the speaker examined historical facts and how they pertained to the present status of African Americans. During his presentation, the speaker discussed the relationship between alcohol and Native peoples. He then connected this to African American males in relationship to the drug problem. At the end of the program (in a school where students were constantly fighting against each other because of different neighborhoods), the students were in tears and vowed to never fight again. One student stated, "In those few hours I learned more than I had been taught in all the years I have been learning history" (Rideau, 1994).

However, immediately following the program, a group of White teachers were reported to have called the school district to inform them that there would be trouble at the school as a result of the Black History program. The next day, the school was surrounded with school board personnel, sheriff deputies, and newspaper reporters. The headline of the local newspaper read "Muslim Stirs Controversy at the School," which implied that the speaker had done something to create controversy ("Controversy at high school," 1994).

The students at this southern school were able to work from level four of the Banks model, which should be the ultimate goal in the implementation of Black History—a Black History program that meets the expectations of its founder, Carter G. Woodson.

The growing diversity in American schools demands more than just an addition of various ethnic groups into the curriculum; it also requires serious truth telling. This truth telling must be grounded in issues of justice and equity. At the core of educating for diversity is Black History. The history of multicultural education grew out of the struggle of African Americans seeking equity and justice in the American society. It is unfortunate that the opponents of Black History and multicultural education believe it will cause divisiveness in the society. Opponents of diversity should observe that there is unity in diversity, which is demonstrated when observing flowers in a garden. All of the flowers grow in a common soil and need water for their survival. In the same way we all seek freedom, justice, and equality.

As demonstrated, it is difficult to predict when or even if the controversy surrounding Black History will end. But it is important to understand that educators, parents, and students play a vital role in ensuring that the mis-education ends. In the next chapter, we examine through case study the controversy around this Black history program and other factors such as racism and its role in the education of African Americans.

Chapter 4

Racism in School

The purpose of this chapter is to give the reader insight into the school controversy and student protest centered on a Black History Program in a Louisiana school. The chapter is divided into three main parts: 1) Black Student Protest in Louisiana, 2) Controversy at Central High School: The Black History Program, and 3) Student Protest at Central High School[1].

The case study approach is considered a *bounded system*, which means that it is bounded by time and place: "it is the case being studied a program, an event, an activity, or individuals" (Patton, 1990). In this book, the case study format will provide the reader with a background of the activities that have shaped the experiences of student activists.

There are multiple sources of information which must be used when doing a case study (Patton, 1990). This study employed the following sources: information, observation, interviews, audio-visuals, newspapers, and public documents.

A very important aspect of the case study is shaping the context of the case (Patton, 1990). The context of a case could be its historical, physical, or social setting. This study uses a historical approach for the shaping of the context. The history of Black student protest in Louisiana is used to provide a historical chronology of events that have taken place in Louisiana.

---

[1] It should be noted that in the section Controversy at Central High School, and the sections that follow, pseudonyms are used to protect the confidentiality of the participants.

Black Student Protest in Louisiana

There were many instances in Louisiana in which African Americans had to protest for equal treatment. It was common during the late 1960s and early 1970s for Black student protest to center around the desire for more knowledge in Black Studies. Many of these early student protests revealed the racist policies of colleges and schools throughout Louisiana.

One case took place at Southern University in New Orleans, where students removed the American flag and replaced it with a flag that was Black, green, and gold. The students took it a step further by pledging allegiance to the Black, green, and gold. The pledge was as follows:

> I pledge allegiance to the Black Liberation Flag and to the cause for which it stands. Black people together indivisible for liberation, self-defense, self-determination. I am prepared to give my life in its defense (Murray, 1978, p. 13).

During the late 1960s and early 1970s, actions such as these were occurring throughout America. African American students from New York to San Francisco were brandishing guns and demanding courses in Black Studies. Some of the southern Black colleges were patrolled by the National Guard and on some campuses, African American students were shot to death (Fairclough, 1995).

At Southern University, Black student protest resulted in the death of two students, Denver Smith and Leonard Brown (Davis, 1997). Such situations were not confined to only college campuses; there were several high schools in the state of Louisiana that had Black student protests. At many high schools, student protest was centered on desegregation issues. In 1969 at Alcee Fortier High School in New Orleans, Black students protested when the principal refused to accept the Black students' demands for a Black student union. The protest and picketing of the school entrances resulted in the arrest of 80 demonstrators (Britton, 1969).

A similar protest took place in Iberia Parish in 1970, but the racial situation was much more violent. On the opening day of school, students from Jennarette High began fighting. Three days later, after a Black girl was expelled for striking a White teacher, Black students left the school and tried to march to their old school, which had been downgraded to a junior high (Fairclough, 1995). The students were confronted by the police force, resulting in a clash involving rock throwing and tear gas. In 1972, Jennerette High would be the scene of another student protest; this time, Black students protested the election of a White homecoming queen. The protest resulted in 40 Black students being suspended, whereas others were expelled for four years.

Black students at Bogalusa High School also protested the homecoming activities. The controversy began in October 1969 when there were no Black students on the homecoming court. When Blacks walked out of school, the judge ordered that they immediately return to school. The controversy soon escalated when a disturbance occurred at a football game, resulting in the expelling of Black students and creating more racial tensions. On one occasion, about six hundred students engaged in a free for all during recess; police in riot gear were rushed to the high school campus (Fairclough, 1995).

In Abbeville and Vermillion Parishes, Black students walked out in October of 1971 because of a homecoming dispute. This conflict resulted in a riot two months later. One of the more violent student protests took place in 1974 at Destrehan High School in St. Charles Parish, when a Black student was arrested and convicted of killing a White student (Fairclough, 1995). Many of the racial problems in public schools were due to the fact that many of the Black teachers were regarded as incompetent. The National Teachers Examination was one of the tools used to replace Black teachers within the educational system. As one Black lawyer stated:

> The Whites have the power. The power to call Black teachers what they want to call them. And in a lot of cases they call them incompetent. Now I'm not saying that 100 percent of Black teachers who come through my office are competent. But it sure is strange that I haven't heard of any White teachers displaced because of incompetence (p. 446).

Between 1966 and 1971, the number of White teachers employed in public schools increased to over 4,000, while the number of Black teachers increased to only 650 (1995). Added to this racial problem in the public school system was that during the period of 1966 to 1971, there was a large decline in Black principals, while the number of White principals increased (Butler, 1974).

In St. Landry Parish in the spring of 1987, one of the largest African American student protests occurred in the state of Louisiana. This protest took place as a result of the school board's decision to consolidate the parishes' predominantly African American high schools. The building sites of the new schools were approved in areas where the majority of the residents were White. Property was being donated by a Black organization to keep the schools in the African American neighborhood; however, the board refused to accept the offer of $1 per acre ("Site vote protested," 1987). The school board decided to purchase land in the Prairie Rhode area for $100,000 per acre. This decision outraged the Black communities, because the board rejected the forty-acre site that was offered by an African American organization in Lafayette. Individuals in the African American communities felt this action showed the blatant racism of many of its school board members.

The protest of the school board action started with the students at Plaisance High School. Organization of the student protest took place three days in advance with several student leaders meeting at the home of a teacher (Pitre, personal experience, 1987). The students at this meeting met with community leaders and decided what type of strategy should be planned to protest the school board's decision. On Friday morning, the student protest began when students walked out of class. Several of the students expressed their disgust with the school board's decision by expressing concern about the school's heritage, noting that their parents attended classes there also. Despite having little material to work with, the students said they had one of the best schools in the parish ("Rally to protest school sites," 1987).

On March 24, 1987, Luther Hill, the Parent Teacher Organization (PTO) president in the Palmetto area said, "The St. Landry school board did something we've been trying to do for the last 15 years. You've awakened us from our sleep" ("Site vote protested," 1987). Over 1,000 African Americans discussed the school consolidation issue at the Holy Ghost Catholic Church. With such an enormous crowd, there were people standing outside of the church, resulting in the placement of speakers on the outside. One of the speakers suggested that a boycott of local businesses as well as forcing the resignation of some school board members was the method to employ. While the meeting was taking place, several Opelousas Police Department cars arrived at Holy Ghost Catholic Church. Father McKnight, Priest of Holy Ghost Catholic Church, and Joshua Pitre, School Board Member, were confronted by policemen who explained that there was a bomb threat and the bomb would go off in 15 minutes (Pitre, J., personal communication, June 1997). Despite the threat, the meeting was a success as African Americans remained steadfast in their quest for justice. At this meeting, the St. Landry Parish protest received national attention when Dan Rather of CBS aired the meeting on his evening show.

On March 25, 1987, over 50 protesters met with the school board. Among those protesting were Willie Pitre, a local pastor, Samson Robinson, a parent, and Luther Hill, president of the Palmetto PTO. Hill stated that one of the primary goals would be the use of an economic boycott ("Board office picketed," 1987). Economic measures would come later as the next major form of protest resulted when African American teachers held a sick-out. This tactic, along with student protest, forced many of the schools to close down on March 26, 1987. In Plaisance, police were dispatched when students threatened to burn the building. At Opelousas High School, 15 teachers did not show up for work. In Lawtell, six teachers failed to show up ("Teachers stage sickout," 1987).

The African American student protest movement became confrontational when protesters entered the St. Landry school board office. Thirty-four demonstrators were arrested when they took over the board's office for several hours ("Protesters enter office," 1987). State troopers and sheriff deputies were called to the scene when protesters refused to leave. Palmetto teacher Augusta Rideau, one of the demonstrators, read a list of demands the African American community desired. Among the demands were that the two new parish high schools be located in the predominantly Black communities of Plaisance and Grand Couteau and that Black builders should receive half the school construction business, and Black educators half the administrative positions in the school system ("Protesters enter office," 1987). There were protesters inside as well as outside the school board office. Meanwhile, state troopers were positioned on the Creswell exit waiting for orders to move in. When protesters were asked to leave and they refused, state troopers moved in, and many of the protesters were hit with batons.

Policemen began dragging and kicking protesters, several of whom were injured during the attempt to remove them from the school board's entrances. In the parking lot, a school board worker hit James Leblanc as he attempted to leave the scene. A woman identified as Frances Thibodeaux was injured by police and taken to the Opelousas General Hospital. Vernon White, one of those arrested for entering the school board building, was injured when he was pushed from behind. As White lay on the ground in obvious pain, many protesters began shouting at the policemen. Among the people arrested was Father McKnight, priest at Holy Ghost Catholic Church of Opelousas, one of the largest African American catholic churches in America. McKnight was later charged with enticing juveniles to violate the law and obstructing the entrance to a public building. According to policemen, McKnight was on a bullhorn ordering protesters to resist arrest ("Protestors enter office,"1987). McKnight, in his autobiography *Whistling in the Wind,* stated that the police had intended to arrest him before they arrived at the school board meeting. According to McKnight, a young man told him that he had been monitoring the State Police radio and had heard that the latter were going to arrest McKnight (Moore, 1988). McKnight stated:

> When the officer spotted me he cried out "There's McKnight!" He lunged toward me but was stopped by their commander. Soon afterwards they started to remove those blocking the entrance, and the turmoil erupted. I got on the bullhorn and told the crowd to stay calm. Immediately the commander of the state police issued the order to arrest me. I was roughly seized by several officers, who knocked the bullhorn out of my hands and threw me against the car. My arms were pulled behind my back and handcuffed. I was then taken to the back seat of a city police car with two others. We sat squeezed in close quarters for quite some time (p. 70).

One of the 34 people arrested was the athletic director at Plaisance High School, Murphy Guillory. He explained his reason for protesting by saying,

"I was protesting where the school board voted to put the school. We're not protesting them closing our school down. I can't see why the school board wants to put a school in mud and water and leave a first class place they could have had for one dollar an acre" ("Plaisance coach among group arrests," 1987).

In a final attempt to get justice, more than 500 African American protesters held a march from Holy Ghost Catholic Church to the school board, then back to the Holy Ghost Catholic Church behind a coffin symbolizing their determination to bury racism. McKnight, according to the White leadership, was disrupting the racial harmony that was perceived to exist. In a letter to Father McKnight, Bishop Harry Flynn expressed his opinion about the student protest:

> No matter how worthy the cause, the Church decries and must speak out against any demonstration, speech or activity which may be considered inflammatory or which may promote or provoke violence. The involvement of young people in activities which may be harmful to them or to others cannot be condoned. (Moore, 1988)

Eventually, the St. Landry school board made some concessions to the African American community. Those concessions consisted of having African American principals at schools that were majority African American and having at least one African American assistant principal at all of the schools in the parish. In those areas where African Americans were extremely poor and had very little representation, the school board refused to provide equal services to such schools. The primary lack of service was reflected in the curriculum and transportation of students who participated in extra-curricular activities.

The next major controversy in Louisiana occurred as the result of a Black History Program. The events that followed the Black History Program resulted in a student protest that made state news for several days.

Controversy at Central High School

Central High School is located in the northeastern part of Laurel Parish in Levy, Louisiana, which is located about 50 miles from Alexandria, Louisiana and approximately 45 miles from the state capital in Baton Rouge. In the early years of the civil rights movement in America, Levy served as one of the first examples of what could take place when African Americans united. In 1950, one evening in the sweltering heat of June, Blacks gathered in a small church in the tiny hamlet of Levy, Louisiana to hear a distinguished guest speaker talk to them about Democracy.

During this meeting, Alvin Jay, a former school teacher, and executive secretary of the New Orleans Urban League, reminded Blacks that they did not have a single person registered to vote in Laurel Parish. When Jay attempted to get people to register to vote by going to the courthouse in Central South, he was assaulted by a group of Whites. Alvin Jay stated, "I was slugged with the butt of a gun and pounded with a pair of brass knuckles." During this confrontation, Jay's head was punctured with some type of object. "They left a hole in my head," Jay recounted. In an interview, with an individual who brought Jay to a local physician, the interviewee stated it looked like someone had tried to scalp Jay. Eighteen months later, Jay died, possibly from the blow that he suffered in Levy.

Laurel Parish had been regarded by many as one of the worst places for Blacks to reside. It was an area in which Whites were sternly against equality for Blacks. A local priest told Black civil rights lawyer A.P. Tureaud that Whites in Laurel Parish were immovably opposed to Black voting. Forty-five years later, Levy would stimulate the conscious of African Americans throughout the Acadiana area.

History of Central High School

In 1989, the Laurel Parish School Board approved that a consolidated school be placed in Levy. The consolidated school opened in 1990 and was comprised of students that formerly attended Walker, Carter, Wheatley, and Dunbar High Schools. With the combination of different schools attending Central, the first years were marked with extensive fighting among students.

In 1991, Mervyn Anderson was appointed principal at the newly created school. Several measures were taken by Mr. Anderson to curtail many of the problems that confronted the school. In the initial stages, Mr. Anderson began by looking for young teachers who could impact the students in a positive manner. In the fall of 1992, George Herbert, a student teacher from Southern University, was assigned to Central High School. Herbert's assignment was to teach Free Enterprise and American History under the supervision of Huey Kinister. The first week of Herbert's assignment was to observe Mr. Kinister's classes.

Herbert would state that his first days at Central were a learning experience. During this time, he noticed the mediocre concern of the students toward learning history. In particular, the students did not have any knowledge of the accomplishments of Black people. The following days would find Herbert teaching the class. There were times, he would wonder how he would fare as a teacher. In the beginning Herbert was very nervous about what he would say and wondered how he would keep the students involved for an entire hour. He also felt kind of strange, because many of the students were not much younger than he was. This would eventually change as time passed. However, Herbert was confronted with some of the problems of the school when he overheard a group of students discussing their plans to fight at the Friday night football game. Herbert did not report it to the principal because he thought that would have been an improper thing to do. Instead, he lectured on the historical subjects of how ignorance leads to people of the same condition to fighting one against the other. As time progressed, the students at Central were introduced to a new way of learning history.

After George Herbert's semester of student teaching was up, he continued to work with the students. Although the first two years of consolidation marked a period of poor test results for students at Central, when the 1991-92 school year was over Central students showed a tremendous improvement in their exit exam scores. During this same year, the Central High School history department put together its first student council. It was a year in which the Booster Club was predominantly White, even though the school consisted of over 80 percent African American students. At the close of the 1991-92 school year, Central had begun the process of developing a school that would rank among the best in Laurel Parish.

The 1992-93 school year found Central with at least two new teachers. Among those teachers was Mr. George Herbert, who had just recently graduated from Southern University. It was Mr. Anderson's idea to hire Mr. Herbert since he had done such a tremendous job in bringing up the exit exam scores at the school the previous year. During the first month of Mr. Herbert's stay at Central, he was appointed as assistant football coach. His primary job was to coach the eighth grade sports. Since Central had just begun its football program, the team was not very good. The first two years had witnessed the team suffer losses of every game on the junior high level.

Not only was the new school plagued with athletic problems, but it was also plagued with academic problems. The list of academic problems included low grades on report cards and very little participation in parish contests. These contests involved the Social Studies Fair, the Science Fair and other academic activities.

In his first day in the classroom, Mr. Herbert laid down the class rules. Herbert knew exactly what he intended to get out of his students. He was excited because Central was a majority Black school and also provided an opportunity for him to develop students who were in some people's eyes un-redeemable and unworthy of any type of valuable education. One of the students recalled her first experience in Mr. Herbert's class: "I hated it, I was very scared, because he seemed mean." She recalls that Mr. Herbert said, "This is not going to be like the rest of your classes where you sit down and do nothing, you're going to work. And if you don't want to work you get your bag and get your schedule changed. When he said that I knew I would have to get out of that class." Herbert's no-nonsense philosophy would eventually be viewed as the key to establishing a strong educational foundation for many of his students.

On the football field, Central's eighth grade team would lose only two games during the 1992 season. This marked a dramatic turnaround for the junior high program. It was difficult at first because on his first day of observing the players, Herbert noticed that their pants were sagging. It was as though they were trying to be cool. He told them it was going to be "my way or the highway." His philosophy was "winning is not everything it is the only thing." This philosophy was no doubt valuable, as yielded positive results. Herbert, because of his athletic accomplishments, would be asked to direct Central High School's Black History Program.

Black History Program

The first controversy at Central High occurred as the result of a Black History Program in February of 1993. This program received negative criticisms because it was poorly planned. While the guest speaker was in the middle of his lecture, the bell sounded to dismiss students from school. Instead of the students sitting and waiting for further instructions, they walked out of the auditorium, leaving the guest speaker standing at the podium. Principal Anderson received criticism for his appointment of those individuals in charge of the Black History Program.

The following school year, Mr. Anderson appointed George Herbert to be in charge of putting the Black History Program together. Initially, Herbert didn't know what to do because he had never before organized a Black History Program. Immediately after his appointment, Herbert began consulting students and teachers about the mistakes made in the previous program. Finally it was decided that the Student Council along with Mr. Herbert would find a guest speaker that would be different from traditional guest speakers. The decision was made to get a speaker from the Nation of Islam.

Herbert remarked about the decision, "Initially we knew nothing about the Nation of Islam; it was probably Malcolm X who all of us knew more about." In early January, Alfred Muhammad was asked to be the guest speaker at this event. Once he accepted the invitation, the program was well on its way to being a success. The day before the program, Mr. Herbert assigned a group of young men to help keep order during the program. Many of these young men were considered the troublemakers in the school. On the day of the program, only a few people knew who the speaker would be. When Alfred Muhammad arrived on the campus, he was met by at least 25 young men dressed in suits and ties. The majority of the faculty was shocked by the simple fact that these young men were dressed up. Muhammad's lecture would cause the first major controversy at Central High School.

Controversy after Black History Program

Immediately following Muhammad's lecture, a group of White teachers was reported to have called the school board and informed them of fighting among students because of the Black History Program. The next day, the school was surrounded with school board personnel, sheriff deputies, and newspaper reporters. On February 25, 1994 the *Daily News Advertiser* front page column read, "Muslim stirs controversy at High School." While this article seems to give the idea that the guest speaker was the primary reason for the controversy, this was not true. The controversy began when a few White teachers became upset about the content of Mr. Muhammad's speech.

Many of the students expressed their feelings about Mr. Muhammad and the program. Charles Lester, a White student who was present, discussed his interpretation of the lecture: "He put down on the Lord, It was very insulting I don't blame nobody for this, just the man for what he said." According to Lester, several teachers walked out during the assembly and he and his friend were also tempted to do the same thing. "He just put down on all the religions," said James Poterman, Lester's friend who was also waiting to leave school. "When he started to put down on religion, Charles and I looked at each other and said we are about to walk out."

The African American students, on the other hand, voiced a different opinion about the situation. "I think the program was actually wonderful," said Hope Lagrange, Student Council President. "He did not come up with any off the wall stuff . . . He had done his research." At least three students who spoke with the media agreed with Stephanie Wilhite, a 17-year old who stated, "The man just spoke the truth. He said he could prove it and he gave names, dates, and times when it all began. I think it was a misunderstanding on the part of White students. . . . He didn't just talk about just White people." While some of the White students said the speech was offensive, Shonta Callister, a Black student, stated, "He really didn't say nothing to offend them . . . I think they just want to complicate the whole situation." According to some of the Black students, White students in Laurel Parish public schools have a tendency to check out of school before the Black History Program.

At Central West High School, a similar incident was reported a few days later. The headline of the *Daily News Advertiser* newspaper read "Central West Students Protest." This time Black students walked out because of the lack of respect that White students had for Black History. Vince Spocke, Student Body President, and Shamil Spurlock, parliamentarian for the senior class, were leading the student movement. Spocke said they felt they were being disrespected by White students who did not attend the Black History Program. The principal at

Central West acknowledged the fact that "it is common for White students not to attend Black History assemblies."

Despite such problems, the Laurel School Board asked the principal at Central to make an apology for the remarks of Mr. Muhammad. On February 27, 1994, the *Daily News Advertiser's* front page read "School Plans Apology for Speaker." The paper stated that an apology would be made on Monday. The principal was being asked to make an apology by the school board personnel, but in particular by school board member Lori Geege. Geege would reveal, "I talked to the principal and he told me there would be an investigation and a public apology would be made to the students and the public." Several Black students and parents were upset over the fact that the principal would apologize for the truth. Mr. Anderson was not present for the Black history program and before an investigation into the matter was completed he agreed to an apology. The Black parents and students believed that pleasing the White community was more important than accepting the truth.

Many of the White parents reacted to the actions of a few teachers who left the program. One White parent stated that her child came home upset about the program. The parent stated, "What was bad was that the Black teachers cheered him on. We have to get along at this school. We don't want racial problems in our school. It is just causing trouble." School board member Lori Geege responded with, "Parents were upset by an outsider coming in and in their opinion, was trying to divide the Whites and Blacks in District 5 . . . There is great respect between Blacks and Whites in this community. I too feel that it is unfortunate that outside forces made an attempt to destroy the relationship between Blacks and Whites . . . this type of Black History Program, which was organized by the Student Council and teacher advisor George Herbert, would have been more appropriate for college students rather than high schoolers."

In response to the White community's statements, the Black community formed a group called Concerned Parents. The chairperson of the organization was Kathy Pios. In an attempt to get to the source of the controversy, the organization asked for the resignation of all those teachers that walked out of the program. The resignation of the principal was also requested because of the apology he made without having full knowledge of what took place.

Teacher-Student Confrontation

The controversy escalated even more when a Black student and one of the White teachers who stirred the controversy got into a fight. The *Daily News Advertiser* printed on its front page on March 22, 1994, "Central Teacher Attacked by Student." Anthony Wofford, the teacher who was supposedly attacked, stated, "I was on lunch duty recess, and there were some students hitting or kicking one of the doors. I walked over to investigate and made a general statement, not to anyone specifically, that you need to stop kicking the door or you are going to break it." Wofford later heard another strike on the door. This time, Wofford approached the crowd again but placed particular emphasis on one particular student, Toni Green. Wofford would state about Green, "He walked off like I wasn't even speaking to him. At that point, I said I was going to have to write him up for disrespect." According to Wofford, Green braced up to him and asked, "Did you see me kick the door?" Immediately following this incident, Wofford requested that the administration remove Green from the campus.

Later in the day, the actual confrontation between Green and Wofford took place. Wofford stated that he heard the student say, "If he is a man, he will come out." Wofford also stated that when he did step out of the classroom, the assault began. "As soon as I stepped out into the hall to take the duty post, he grabbed me by the arm and threw me on the floor and I just went limp." Wofford went to the Central South General Hospital after the incident. The Laurel Parish Sheriff's Office conducted an investigation into the incident to find out what actually took place. "We are waiting for Mr. Wofford to come in and give the complete details, said Laura Bemmini, chief criminal deputy for the Sheriff's Department. We really don't know what happened at this point."

While Wofford expressed his view on the incident, some students who were present stated that Wofford incited the attack by making comments about anyone who seemed to agree with the speaker of the Black History Program. Wofford verified that the real reason behind the incident was his disgust over the Black History Program, admitting that ever since the speech at the Black History Program, he had felt animosity from Black faculty and students at Central. Wofford also made the following comments to his students: "I walked out of the assembly because I found it very insulting. I told the students what I thought about it and I apologized to the Black students . . . because they had to listen to another African American talk like that." One student reported in her opinion that Wofford was at the door saying something to Green. "Then Green ran up to Wofford and grabbed him by the collar, from the back, and snatched him and threw him to the other side of the hall. It seemed as though the air was knocked out of Wofford and as he hit the wall, Wofford uttered, "My words," and then started to slide down the wall. Then Green came up and snatched him by his tie, then he slapped his glasses off his face and they went flying down the hall."

According to this same source, Wofford would use derogatory names toward Black students such as "Jiggaboo, big lip porch monkeys, shine, jungle bunnies and mammys." Lashaya Green, first cousin of Toni Green, stated that she heard Wofford use derogatory statements when talking to one African American student in particular: "He would be funny with Shawn and use names with her, in a joking manner. We could tell it was a difference between the way he treated the Black and White students. White students could call him by his first name." Green further stated that when she asked her cousin why he had the confrontation with Wofford, he indicated that, "Wofford called him a nigger." As a result of the incident between Toni Green and Anthony Wofford, the Concerned Parents organization asked for the removal of the principal and two teachers.

Efforts to Remove Teachers

On March 31, 1994, the front page of the *Daily News Advertiser* read "School Troubles: Parent Wants to Oust Principal, 2 Teachers." Kathy Pios stated that the reason for the removal of the principal Mervyn Anderson was that, "he is not treating things happening over here fairly. . . . He is not standing up for what is right." Pios also stated that they were asking two teachers at the school to resign. "We are asking the two teachers to resign because they are racist. It has happened before and it just got bad after the Black History Program." The two teachers who were asked to resign were Anthony Wofford and Elaine Reed. Many of the parents were extremely upset over the fact that Toni Green was expelled from school despite racial slurs made by Wofford. According to those parents, the student was provoked by racial slurs made by the teacher.

In an effort to remove those teachers, the Concerned Parents Organization wrote a letter to the Laurel School Board. This letter, dated April 5, 1994, expressed the major concerns for the removal of Wofford and Reed:

Daily we are asked to lead our children in choosing the path to be educated, corrected and accept adult guidance and leadership. Each morning we coax, praise, and pray that our children will enter the realm of learning in their classrooms, hoping they will be productive for that day and prepare themselves to be better people for the future. However, in the past few months we begun to question choices of leadership when a simple Black History Program was labeled as not beneficial because a chosen few unintelligent people chose to leave the audience, not accepting historical facts and comparisons for their true value. Can we change history? In life we have learned we must study history for the sake of not repeating its mistakes. The reign of Hitler, the bombing of Hiroshima, the bondage of slavery are some of the cruel events of history. Why not tell our children Black and White the actualities of reality.

Racism was and is the basis used in past historical events that caused races to be intimidated and deprived of human dignity. Why should we repeat history that is destructive to mankind. There are a chosen few who have failed to rise above the level of making differences and continue to intimidate students by using derogatory terms we feel should not exist in any part of our educational system. If our instructors begin to use separatism and racism in identification and procedures in the classroom at Central as Mr. Wofford and Mrs. Reed have, we feel this should not and will not be the accepted norm.

We feel that due the severity of their action and behavior, we demand their immediate voluntary resignation as instructor at Central High School. Should they elect not to voluntarily resign, then we are demanding that the school board immediately remove them before their contagious racism infect other employees and most importantly our children. We sincerely suggest if any other educator or member of the system has chosen to be a negative force in the learning process, he or she need to take hold of the actual purpose of their profession and what it entails more study of the ramification of the Constitution....

All men are created equal, etc. . . .

With best wishes together we can transform our bitter and ugly past into a future where our ideas of our constitution would be made a reality for all.

With pressure mounting and the situation becoming intensified there was a meeting among the ministers of the community. In the meeting, Wofford's minister, Mr. May, suggested that Wofford would leave Central if he could get Herbert suggesting that Wofford would leave only if Herbert was removed.

The NAACP supported the parents in this effort to remove Wofford and Reed. Several NAACP officials were present at the Black History Program. Luther Hillstock, president of the Laurel Parish NAACP, expressed his feelings about the situation by saying, "The system is racist for allowing those type of things to happen . . . We met with the superintendent last year about White teachers leading White students out of those programs." Hillstock also stated that the Laurel School Board had been approached about implementing a policy that would deter this type of behavior. "We approached the superintendent a week prior to the assembly and asked that a policy be established."

The battle over the removal of these two teachers was successful. Wofford took a leave and Reed was transferred to Central East. The controversy took another turn, as it turned out to be a "war of the pen." Both sides began writing newspaper editorials describing their feelings about the situation that occurred at Central. There were four letters detailing attitudes and beliefs about the controversy.

Letters to the Editor

One letter written by a student, entitled "Another View on Central," expressed a positive attitude about the entire Central controversy. The student stated that this program did not divide the communities." As far as separating the two communities, we were never united, totally, we simply tolerate each other. The only thing that will completely sever the ties between the Black and White communities is a certain group of people who continue to pursue this issue in a negative way." In explaining the value of the Black History Program, the student stated, "I would also like to thank Mr. George Herbert for bringing Brother Muhammad to Central. In those few hours I learned more than I had been taught in all the years I have been learning about history." If this is true, then it would serve community leaders well to investigate what is being taught in the public schools of Laurel Parish.

The second letter to the editor took a significant twist, as the athletic director was implicated as one of the teachers that walked out of the program. In this letter to the editor, Richard P. Stelly discussed how many of the teachers at Central were racist and that with such attitudes they should work in other schools like ABW and Belmont:

> We have some racist teachers in our public schools, those who send their children to private schools because a Black teacher isn't good enough to teach their children, but they teach ours. Well, let those teachers go to A.B.W., Belmont and teach at those schools. There they don't have to worry about a Black History Program.

In the second part of the letter, Stelly pointed out that the athletic director walked out of the Black History Program. He then revealed an incident in which the athletic director allowed his players to play in a game in which they were called racial epithets:

> Now to close out this matter, head coach Jack Feiner also walked out of the program. I recall last fall he took his football team to Buckeye High School, which is all White. After one of their players got injured tackling a CHS player, bedlam broke loose. His players had to listen to racial slurs and fight the rest of the game. There were fans for Buckeye trying to get in the fight and all, and this, I must say, had great chances of turning into a riot. Did Coach Feiner walk off the field with his players? Did he ask for an apology from the coach or principal from Buckeye? Was this matter reported to LHSAA? No, it just blew over and the only thing we saw was CHS defeat Buckeye.

A letter defending Coach Jack Feiner stated that the coach had the right to leave a program that he did not like. It went further to state that "Coach Feiner cares about his players. What would he have accomplished by taking his players off the field but depriving them of their first district win?"

In his defense, Coach Jack stated he walked out of the program because he had a prior commitment. "I, along with an assistant left the assembly early because of a previously scheduled commitment and meeting with coaches from Central South Catholic concerning a basketball game as it pertained to the officials, schedule, etc." This may have been a valid reason for Coach Feiner leaving the program; however, his actions still warranted questioning, since White teachers have been known to lead White students out of Black History Programs.

Principal Hearing

On August 10, 1995, a special meeting was held by the Laurel School Board to decide whether to renew the contract of Central's Mervyn Anderson. Anderson was charged with violating 10 of the Laurel School District's School Board Policies. Anderson countered that many of the charges were racially motivated. The basis of one of the charges against Anderson was that he did not act properly after the school's first Black History Program. Superintendent Raymond Feiner told Anderson that George Herbert should be transferred from his position.

After both sides gave opening statements, they presented the witnesses they would call. One of the charges levied against Anderson was that he failed to attend a scheduled program on February 26, 1993, and proper respect was not given to the assembly presenter. This resulted in students leaving because the bell sounded to dismiss school for the day. Immediately following the program, there were no school board personnel at the school to investigate why students left the speaker standing. It was dismissed as just bad timing. This charge was upheld and Anderson was found liable.

Another charge levied against Anderson was that his failure to keep staffing appointments created difficulty for those involved in the staffing procedure. In his defense, Jacqueline Jones testified that she stopped Anderson as he was leaving the campus to inform him that a student was coming to the campus with a gun to kill her son. This was one of the three charges of which Anderson was cleared. The seven remaining charges were as follows:

- Charge 1. While employed by the Laurel Parish School Board, and while in the course and scope of employment as principal of Central High School, you violated the Laurel Parish bookkeeping policies.

- Charge 3. On or about November 30, 1992 while employed by the St. Landry Parish School Board, and while in the course and scope of your employment, an internal audit of the books of Central High School revealed books not in balance and internal control problems. Deficiencies were found in receipts disbursements, fund raisers and athletic gate proceeds.

- Charge 4. On February 26, 1993 while employed by the St. Landry Parish School Board, you failed to attend a scheduled assembly program.

- Charge 5. On or about August 10, 1994 while employed by the Laurel Parish School Board, you neglected instruction from Mr. Drew Diaz, Assistant Superintendent, to send a faculty representative to a workshop to learn of a new program to be presented to all schools. By your school not having representation at this workshop, special arrangement had to be made to provide the information on grade level Teaching Kits to all faculty members, creating a burden on the school system as well as the local personnel for the American Cancer Society.

- Charge 6. On August 1, 1994 you failed to remit payment for Central High School's athletic insurance. Notice was sent to you January 3, 1995 by Mr. Rado, Supervisor, that as of that date the insurance payment still was not made.

- Charge 9. You were notified after an audit of your 1994-95 school records, that there were policy violations and/or irregularities of 15 cumulative records and 9 teacher grade books.

- Charge 10. On or about May 19, 1994 and May 11, 1995. The 1994 evaluation showed lack of support for board policy, and the need to attend all school activities. The rating scale showed needs improvement. The 1995 evaluation also showed lack of support of board policy, and rating scale showed needs improvement. The total points and average decreased from 1994 to 95.

Of the charges levied against Anderson none mentioned the controversy surrounding the Black History Program on February 24, 1994[2].

---

[2] This was probably done purposely because the real reason behind Anderson's dismissal was the fact that the school board had, under the order of Judge Harriet, reinstated Raymond Duhoss, who had been previously fired from his position as principal of Central South High School. Central South High now had two principals. Although the judge had ordered reinstatement, there was no stipulation that Duhoss had to stay at Central South an entire year. The board seized upon this opportunity and later transferred Duhoss to Central High School. Duhoss would state that the transfer was not anything he asked for and said his lawyer felt the school board was not in compliance with the ruling that said he had to be reinstated at Central South High School.

Principal Fired

In the final analysis, Anderson was fired from his job as principal of Central High School. The board voted 8-4 not to renew Anderson's contract. Board member Lori Geege, who is the representative of Central District, voted to have Anderson removed. Geege also made the motion to have Anderson dismissed. Anderson stated that Lori Geege told him that she would support him if he had all his documents together. Prior to Anderson being selected as principal he had campaigned for Geege. Anderson would later say that he didn't know what he had done to get out of Geege's favor.

Football Player Walkout

Immediately following the board's decision to fire Mervyn Anderson, football players boycotted the first days of practice. On August 14 and 15, the *Daily News Advertiser* ran articles discussing the athletic walkout by several of the Central football players. It wasn't until about August 20, 1995 that the players began to return to practice. One of the organizers of the boycott, Kathy Pios, stated that in the four years that Jack Feiner had been here, no scholarships have been given out. She would further state that the players were talented enough to receive scholarships. Jack Feiner agreed that many of his players were talented; however, they were not able pass the ACT, and some of them didn't have the grades to merit scholarships. Pios countered, "A good coach looks out for his kids and makes sure they take the ACT. I asked Jack Feiner if he knew they could take the ACT in the ninth grade and he said he didn't know that." An article in the *Daily News Advertiser*, "Coach Walks Miles for Dubois," outlined how George Herbert had received a scholarship for Herbert Dubois. This article showed the incompetence of Jack Feiner's efforts to receive football scholarships. It is believed that Feiner contacted Superintendent Ryan Feiner and athletic supervisor James Rado, complaining that Herbert was behind the football player walkout.

Transfer of Teacher

On Monday, August 14, 1995, a letter was placed in Herbert mail box informing him that he would be transferred from Central High School. School had already begun, and teachers were reporting to school. In a later school board meeting on August 17, 1995, George Herbert was transferred to Southern High School.

During the August 17, 1995, meeting Mr. Charlie Reed, school board member, objected to Herbert's transfer and appointment. Superintendent Feiner stated that the reason behind Herbert's transfer was that he had interfered with the harmonious operation of Central High School. The board then listened to comments from Ronald Herbert, Social Studies & Foreign Language Supervisor, who stated that such a transfer would be unfair because Herbert had done such a tremendous job at Central. James Rado then asked the board to speak. Herbert, according to Rado, had been involved in the recent student protest concerning the football players. Immediately following Rado's comments, a vote was taken before a capacity-filled school board meeting. The vote was 8–5 as the school board voted in favor of the transfer. While the vote was being taken, Kathy Pios and several other spectators began to disrupt the meeting by shouting. Police from the Central South Department were called to the school board meeting.

Community Reaction

Many of the community leaders were outraged at the action taken by the board. Parish NAACP President Luther Hillstock said the school board continued to practice racist hiring policies. Hillstock went on to say that the board members had hired teachers from predominantly White private schools to teach at CHS and that they should change the name of Central to "KKK Academy." Hillstock recommended looking at teacher composition in Black and White schools in Laurel Parish, where the ratio was 50-50 in predominantly Black schools, while it was probably 85-15 in White schools. Furthermore, he recommended looking at the number of Whites hired before African Americans during the opening months of school. "Whites are practically guaranteed a job, whereas African Americans have to wait for what is available," Hillstock stated. "You have two systems—a White and Black system. Elementary administrators are bringing in White teachers to 80 percent African American schools. By the time African American students reach the seventh and eighth grade they are ready to drop out of school." The board thought that Herbert's transfer would end the controversy at Central, despite the newly appointed principal's warning that such a move was not proper because it did not give him the opportunity to select the personnel he wanted at his school.

Within the three-year period that Herbert was at Central, he implemented a Boys to Men to program, received two football scholarships and one academic scholarship at the school, and helped to start African American studies courses in Laurel Parish. In a school where fighting was common, he helped to bring communities together. During the 1994-95 school year, Central had one of the highest overall scores on the exit exam in the parish. At the Laurel Parish Social Studies Fair, his students received more honors than any other school in the parish. The junior high football team went undefeated for two years, having a re-cord of 21 wins and 2 losses from 1992 to 1994. The eighth grade basketball team was the first to travel out of state to compete in a basketball tournament, and at a tournament in Huntsville, Alabama, Central placed first.

Student Protest

On August 24, 1995, students walked out of classes protesting Herbert's transfer to Southern High School. The protesters carried signs that read, "If Mr. Herbert Goes, So Do We!" The *Daily News Advertiser* stated that while at Cen-tral, Herbert had organized a Boys to Men program in which students with prob-lems got together to discuss them or go to the movies. One of the members of the Boys to Men, David Willis, stated that the next Wednesday would be his last day at school. "I used to like the school a lot but since all this happened I feel the school won't be the same until he returns." John Feiner, PTO President, stated that "the kids came to mind. The progress they were making doesn't count for anything. Society was ready to write off these kids and he was willing to fight for them."

The newly elected principal Raymond Duhoss said that he would not deny the students the right to make a statement—he just hoped it wouldn't happen every day. Duhoss said, "I don't encourage this, because you never encourage this sort of thing, but they do have the right to express themselves as long as they do it in a responsible manner." The Rev. Dale Feiner pointed out that both White and Black students participated in the demonstrations. Carolyn Dubois, a parent who was present at the demonstration stated, "I was shocked to see both White and Black students participating."

On August 7, 1995, the Laurel School District school board was filled with protesters who held signs of their disapproval. Picketers once again lined up in front of the Laurel Parish School Board as students from Central High School protested the transfer of George Herbert to Southern High School. The parents and students from Central had organized a group called Parents and Students Organized for Educational Improvement. At their August 7 meeting, the organi-zation expressed their dislike for the injustices at Central. Herbert, according to the group, was a Black man who gave the predominately Black school a good role model and was well liked by the students.

During the meeting, Ryan Feiner, School Superintendent, stated that Her-bert was not certified and had interfered with the harmonious operation of the school. This was not true because at the date of the transfer, Herbert had just completed his certification. School board member Lori Geege stated she went along with the transfer because Herbert was instilling Muslim doctrines into the students. One of the Black board members, Charlie Ross, stated that, "We have created an ill in that community and I think it would ease that ill to reappoint Herbert." A White board member, Jerry Domingo, stated, "If we had a problem with him why transfer? Of if the problem was not that severe why not keep him at the school where he was?" Domingo then requested that the fate of a teacher be decided by the administrator.

Prior to this statement, principal Raymond Duhoss had requested that Herbert remain at the school. When the vote was taken, the board stood by its decision in a 7–4 vote. Lori Geege and Superintendent Feiner were escorted out of the building as parents and students began yelling obscenities at them. Geege was cornered in the board members' room by a group of parents and students. The students were talking to Geege about her decision to transfer Herbert. In the conversation, she was saying that some people had contacted her and asked for the transfer. Kathy Pios then walked in the room and asked Geege to tell her who asked for this transfer. Geege responded that she didn't have to answer to Pios. The police then entered as Pios told Geege, "If I wanted to do something to Lori I would."

In the month of November, Parents and Students for Quality Education sought to recall board member Lori Geege. Kathy Pios was the chairperson of the group, which filed a recall petition with the Registrar of Voters in Laurel Parish. Pios stated several reasons why the group was asking for the recall:

- A lack of representation of the voters and failure to act in the best interests of the children of District 5.

- Failure to assist in the promotion of Black administrators.

- Failure to see accomplishments that directly affect District 5 schools.

- Apparent prejudice against religious viewpoints.

- Failure to speak out against racist viewpoint of school board which adversely affects the schools.

- Failure to support concerns of District 5 parents who have raised issues regarding the racist policy of the hiring and firing of District 5 employees.

-
- Failure to ensure that a proper and thorough investigation took place following the removal of a faculty member at Central High School.

Geege, in response to the petition, stated that she had stood up for the Black community and everyone else in her district and was now being accused of not representing Blacks. Geege then said, "they have to realize that they are not the majority."

In the final analysis, the Laurel School Board stood by its decision. The result was a steady decline of student scores on the exit exam and ACT. The enrollment of students at Central has dropped, forcing school board officials to decide whether it is feasible to keep the school open. At the time of the study the controversy continues as the Laurel School Board was under suit from a parent, who claims that the school board has discriminated against Central because it is a predominantly African American school. The dismissed principal Mervyn Anderson was also filing suit against the School Board. The controversy and student protest at Central High School could turn out to be a major catalyst for change in Laurel Parish.

Summary

Since its inception in 1926, Black History Programs have caused a great debate. Many of the issues around Black History Programs that existed in 1926 continue to exist in the new millennium. The challenge of implementing Black History into the current curriculum is one that is not going away (Banks, 2002). Banks brilliantly alludes to this as being one of the challenges that school districts face. Added to this is the new wave of student protest surrounding issues of diversity (Rhoads, 1998b). While the media has not focused on student protest in the 1990s and the new millennium with the same passion as it did in the 1960s, according to Levine and Cureton (1998), student protest was quite prevalent in the 1990s. Added to this is the fact that very few studies have focused on student activist experiences of this type of phenomenon.

This gap in the literature encouraged us to find out how the student activists at this high school experienced events associated with the Black history controversy and protests. More importantly, we wanted to know how this impacted the student activists' personal lives and their view of the world. Therefore, the present study targeted the phenomena by using a phenomenological study to ascertain what this experience was like for the student activists.

Chapter 5

Protesting Racism and Inequality:
Student Leaders Speak Out

In this chapter, we have included excerpts from and analyses of in-depth interviews that were conducted with student leaders about the controversy and protest that resulted from the Black History Program in Levy. We intentionally allow for the student voice to take center stage in this section, which begins with some background information about the students who participated in this study. In addition, we discuss research findings to parallel the themes that emerged from the student narratives.

Although several individual questions were asked, each student responded to the following standard prompts during the interview:

- How do you remember events associated with the Black History Program and Student Protest?
- What motivated you to engage in protest?
- How did you perceive faculty and staff response to student activism and student protest?
- How has this phenomenon impacted your perspective of the world?

Student Interviews

Janice

Janice is a first generation college student currently completing a Bachelor of Arts degree. After completing the degree, she plans to become a teacher, track coach, and eventually a school principal. Janice's mother completed high school, while her father only managed to complete fourth grade. In her moments of reflection, Janice recalls how poverty burdened her family immensely. On several occasions, the family meal consisted of "only canned beans." As you read Janice's story about how she became a student activist, it is important to reflect on her background.

Q. How do you remember the events associated with the Black History Program and Student Protest?

Well, the thing that separated this program from all the other programs was something that should not have been a controversy in the first place. The program was very interesting and everybody I was associated with told me they got something out of the program. And that was different because, like I said, the programs before were boring and people just didn't want to be there. But this program, the speaker had the attention of the students. And it all started when we noticed students, more so faculty, started walking out of the program and that is how the controversy got started. . . . We figured teachers are role models and you don't just get up and walk out of a Black History Program. I mean, normally in a Black History Program, you could hear, talking. The students were laughing and talking and you know, nobody was paying attention. But I mean in this program people were really listening to what this man had to say. And for them to get up and walk out was disrespect.

. . . Well, after the program was over we went into the lobby and message flies by the speed of light and we heard that somebody had called the news and said that it was going to be a fight, that it was going to be a riot and that wasn't even the case because nobody was fighting or anything and that is what really started the controversy, when those people left out of there and called the news media and said it is going to a big do-how up here because of this man. He is putting down religion and that's where it all started. And that is where the bulk of the problem came from, you know, when people hear something they are going to make it bigger and bigger and that is where a major problem came in, it wasn't so much that they just got up and left, I mean that was a problem, that was a part. Like I said about the disrespect, the real problem came when students started calling their parents and, you know, the media.

I didn't have to walk on campus [the day after the Black History Program], I could see it from off the bus on the highway. I saw the cop lights and all the dogs. The people in suits and ties from the school board office and I knew right then and there that it was blown completely out of proportion, I knew that someone had been saying something that wasn't true. Because the program was a success and there was no reason for the cops to be there unless somebody was fabricating something and that is exactly what had taken place.

Well, it was myself and my best friend and we always sat together on the bus and we had talked about it the day before. But we didn't think it was going to be that much, we thought the man from the newspaper was going to be there asking what had happened, but we saw policeman, and school board members at the school. We got up and ran to the front of the bus and were the first ones, as soon as the doors open, we were the first ones off the bus and we were bombarded with cameras in our faces and dogs on leashes I was furious because we didn't need to talk to anyone we knew what was going on. . . .
. . . you had different, like you had the White students, and you had the Black students. I can recall this one White girl crying because she was, like I have Black friends and I don't know what is going on, and the Black kids were like what is up with this, why is there all this attention, you know? All our school ever got was negative attention and here comes some more. And we just wanted to know why this thing was blown out of proportion, the bell would ring to go to class and there were still two hundred people in the hall.

Someone had told the White parents that the Black students were going to jump on the White students and the White students were going to jump on the Black students. They just thought we were going to be fighting and all of that came from somebody saying something that wasn't true.

Q.   What motivated you to engage in protest?

I'll put it like this: some people didn't like what this teacher was doing to stop these students from fighting. As ironic as it may seem, some people didn't want us to be unified. They wanted us to keep fighting, and keep getting sent home and getting flunked and staying behind and there was always tension around this teacher. Because he was transforming students. Because he was making them do good and have good grades and have pride in themselves. And then after we heard that they transferred the teacher. Now that had something to do with the Black History Program because he was in charge of that. And so they transferred this teacher and I think it was directly related to the Black History Program. Because they didn't want to see Black kids doing well and they transferred this teacher. And that is when a whole riot started. So the after effects of the Black History Program lasted maybe two years over into the transfer of that teacher. And it was always some hush, hush, shoo, shoo, about this teacher. And because he was so compassionate with his students and people were always saying something.

Q.   How did you feel about the teacher being transferred?

I didn't even want to go to school. If it wasn't for my mom and I was a senior I can honestly say I think I would have dropped out of school. If I didn't have people pushing me. I wasn't the only person that felt like that it was a lot of people that felt like that. To have something just snatched away from you like that something that is so good for no reason. It just devastated myself and all my friends that I was affiliated with because the way I felt about this teacher, I know they felt the same way. And you had no motivation it seemed like, what is the point. Why? Because he was the only one that was teaching us anything in the first place. You know I have had teachers tell me I am here to get a check, now if you get it that's good, if you don't that is your business. And he wasn't there for a check, he was really sincere and wanted to see that you had gained something from his class and we did, it was on the faces of his students. You could see a new attitude and when they took him away, it was just horrible. I had friends that dropped out of school and hadn't gone back to this day.

Q. What happened among the students immediately following the teacher's transfer?

Immediately, we began to have petitions signed because our argument at first was if he is so bad, why are you taking him and placing him somewhere else? If he is so horrible why are you taking him and putting him at another school? Why don't you just fire him if your reason for transferring him is true. So we started to get petitions signed to get him to come back and walked out of class. The school board was like the court they were going to decide if he was going to come back to school and we were protesting in front of the school board, almost every day we were in front of the school board office at least twice a week picketing with signs and were sitting in the school board meetings. Organizing ourselves in case we were given the opportunity to say something. We were just protesting and writing letters and trying to get as much media attention as we could to voice our side because what was being told was one side of it.

Q. How has this experience impacted your life?

Well, the program and all that we have been through, it gave me an awareness, to not be so passive and sit back. And accept what people do to you or say to you. You know, you can always go out and read it for yourself and find out more. It has just made me a stronger person, you know, to deal with things that happened in my life. Now, I could look back at those times and pull something positive from that. You know, it made my will stronger, my determination. I know we may have failed in our efforts to get him back at our school, that didn't take away anything , from what we gained from the experience. . . .

. . . it gave me the determination not to just throw my hands up. If it is going to be a fight then we are going to fight, to the end. And we are going to fight until we can't fight anymore. If you believe in something stand behind it, don't just when someone throws the first rock be the first man to duck and run. I mean it's alright to duck as long as you stand back up. It is alright to fall as long as you get up again and don't take things in stride. And say this happened and I am just going to give up. No.

Q. There used to be a lot of territorial fighting among students in your school. How did the Black History Program change that?

Well, by the time that program had come about all of that was put to an end. Because there was a teacher at our school, he was a new teacher, he came straight out of college. And at that time, around 92 or 93 there were territorial fights every day, I mean 15 to 20 people fighting every day. But I mean, when this teacher got there he started to work with the guys who were fighting. And, you know, letting them know that you really don't have anything to be fighting about. And all of that was to be no more, I mean these same guys were at the Black History Program dressed in suits and ties, were from rival communities and they were like walking and talking to each other because they played a major role, a big part in the organization of the Black History Program.

And that is what led us to wanting to have someone from the Nation of Islam [as a guest speaker]. Because these guys they were on to something, one day they were fighting and the next day they were almost holding hands. They were really feeling close to one another and that was culmination of them being able to tolerate one another. They were becoming friends, they were friends. I think a lot of people took something away from the program and for the most part it was a new self-respect. Those guys who had dressed in the suits and who were from town X and town A, who could not get along at the beginning of the year, they were setting an example. Because everybody knew that those guys just couldn't get along and we saw them dressed in ties, suits, and nice shoes. And were standing there with order and discipline. We said, you know, they have something, because any time you can take somebody who's fighting one day and have them cooperating and being friends the next day, you have accomplished something. And I think a lot of people took that away from the program. We don't have to be disorderly, you know, we can get along and we can have pride in ourselves and in our school. It doesn't have to be a ruckus all the time.

I was elated because I was an athlete and before when you went somewhere and you said that you were from this school you almost got laughed at. But when all this started to come about, our school gained more respect. When you said I am from this school, people said, man you better watch out they are tough. They have something going. I was very excited to have anything to with to do with this program and to be affiliated with this school. Because it wasn't anything to be ashamed of anymore, it was something that we took pride in.

Q. What were some of the problems you experienced as a result of your protest for the teacher to return to Central High School?

It was just my mom because, you know, my father didn't live with us and at first my mom was telling me, "You better not get involved with all of that you are fixing to graduate. Just do your work," and as I started to explain to her, she really didn't know the teacher but when she came to meet him, she said . . . I would say, "Mom I'm going to the school board, can I use the car?" And she would say, "Go ahead. If you need to pick up somebody you can," and normally my mom would tell me "If you use my car don't ride nobody else in it but you." And she came to support me because she knew what I was fighting for was worthwhile and I was never the kind of person to follow something that didn't have any kind of meaning. When I showed her that I really felt strongly about this, then she supported me whole heartedly, in my protesting.

Q.   Did anyone try to discourage you from participating in the protest?

Well, there was a lot of pressure; I had family members telling me what they heard about the teacher. And I should not get involved with that I should just go to school and not be involved with all that. And when you go to class you got your teachers telling you all kinds of things and some friends, I don't consider friends now, but some people were like, "Protest? Why, for what?" It was a lot of pressure but it didn't seem like it at the time. Now if you looked back at it, it was a lot of strain, emotionally and physically. We were crying, and holding picket signs, standing outside for three or four hours in the sun. It was definitely a strain but it was worth it.

Q.   How would you say this teacher impacted you?

As a child, I was—I am talking about a young child—I was quiet, to myself, but as I grew older I became more outspoken and even as I grew older around the time of the Black History Program, I grew to be even more outspoken. I was ambitious, I had self-confidence, and before, when I was much younger I was embarrassed and I didn't have much self-confidence. But I can't give the Black History Program all the credit because of a lot that came from this teacher. He taught me that I was a young woman and I needed to respect myself in order to get respect. I can remember the times when I would wear my pants off of my behind. Just like some of the guys would, but when he saw you like that, he would come over and explain to you. He would not just say, "Don't do that;" he would explain to you why and I grew aware of myself. Things that I used to do I didn't do anymore because I had a respect for myself and now as a woman every day I can see a lesson that I have learned from this man. You know, just showing me life's little lessons that you learn, I got a lot of them from him. Now I think that I can do anything that I want to do. You know I don't have any boundaries or limitations unless I set them for myself. It is not anything you can say, [such as] "You can't do this because you are not smart enough"; if I put my mind to it, I can.

Q.   What do you feel that school administrators need to know when implementing a Black History Program into the curriculum?

I would tell them to get input from the students. I mean, you are not having a Black History Program for the teachers. You are having it for the students; that is your whole point in waking up and going to work every day. So that you can make it better for the students to improve their condition. I would definitely tell them to have a relationship with the students and the schools that you govern, don't be the person that's just making the laws and never see the people that it is affecting. Have an active relationship in your school and just remember that you can learn something from the student. Don't go there and think, "I am the boss and this is the way it is going to be." Because people can open your eyes to a lot of things if you let them and I would suggest taking an active role in getting to know the students. These are basically your employers; if the students didn't go to school you don't have a job, and not to say that in a threatening manner. In just an awareness, listen to the students even if it is a D-minus student. If he or she is talking he must have something to say. And try to refine your students-don't just go to work to collect a check.

Janice has used this experience as a motivational tool to help her achieve her goals. She plans to one day have the same impact on young people as this teacher had on her. Janice also wants to become a teacher, so she can give back to children who grew up like her. However, one of her major goals is to become a school administrator where she feels she can have a greater impact. Currently, Janice is one year away from completing a bachelor's degree in Social Studies Education. She often reflects on her family condition and realizes that she must keep striving to be the first in her family to complete college.

Sheila

Sheila is currently attending a technical school, where she plans to complete a degree in computer technology. Shelia's mother completed high school and her farther finished college. She has aspirations to finish school and one day pursue a bachelor's degree. As a child growing up, Sheila says they were extremely poor. She pointed out that they had what she called "the basics but nothing luxurious." When we conducted the interview with Shelia, she did not seem at the outset to be a very vocal person; however, throughout the interview process her intelligence, passion, and new awakening stood out.

Q. How do you remember the events associated with the Black History Program and Student Protest?

What made [this Black History Program] different was the speaker that we had for this particular program emphasized on us as a Black people and the situation that we are in and we need to stand together. To overcome the obstacles that we were placed in and it wasn't by choice that we were in the United States. And we were struggling because of this and because of that, and it wasn't our fault, but that we can't just say, "It's not our fault." We have to stand together and to do something about it. But speakers at the past Black History Programs just mainly emphasized on okay it is important to get an education. And they talked about the Black leaders from the past that stood up for civil rights, but they didn't actually explain that they had to go through this or had to go through that, in order to struggle to get it. They just said, "Okay, yes, they were good people and they helped us out." That was it.

I knew [Whites] felt threatened by what the speaker had said and the teachers probably thought the students were going to start disobeying them all of a sudden. But personally, my friends and the people that got something out of the program, they were not trying to start chaos throughout the school. It wasn't about that; we laughed at them for being scared because, you know, it was just a speaker that was explaining the facts and that's all.

. . . I think the Black students felt like they were being disrespected because the White teachers walked out and the White teachers walked out because they felt that what the speaker was saying wasn't positive. When actually it was the truth and we felt like, "If it is the truth, why should we be kept from the truth?" You know, and we're not like the White students; they have everything they need, they are not socially challenged, or economically challenged, they have a much better percentage rate of people going to college and people succeeding. You know, we felt like, if this is just our month or our day to hear something positive, to do us some good, why should they be upset about it?

Q.   How did you and the other students feel about the teacher being transferred?

Well, the particular teacher they were trying to remove was the only teacher at the school that motivated Black students to really try hard and succeed. And he was the only teacher that taught the students the real background and the struggles that Black people had to go through and the importance of being a strong Black citizen. And I think it really struck a nerve when the students saw they were trying to take him away from us. When he is the only positive teacher that we have in the school to look up to because he was the only one that hit home about being strong Black people. I think they were really offended by and took it serious, took it to heart.

Q.   What happened among the students immediately following the teacher's transfer? What motivated you to engage in protest?

I know for sure some of the athletes and the students in my class, you know. There were really a lot of people who were outspoken and really wanted to get their point across. When the reporters came, everybody was willing to say something on behalf of the teacher [and] they spoke so well and so clear because they really felt the importance of getting their point across. They really wanted the teacher to stay at the school. They didn't want to lose what they waited so long to have in the first place.

Q.   How has this experience impacted your life?

I think I would be kind of narrow-minded [if not for the experience]. I probably wouldn't understand things about Whites and Blacks because I would be blind to a lot of the facts that I was taught by my teacher. And, you know, when certain things that happen to me, you know, the few encounters that I had with White people, I probably would have brushed it off and probably would have thought it is something that just happens. Because, you know, nobody made an issue of it. I guess they were trying to hide from us all the facts that made us understand who we are and why things happen around us.

Yes, I am definitely more outspoken [now] about things that I felt strongly about, I look back at Black History in a totally different way than I did before. Because the way we were taught, our Black History was a totally different experience with the teacher in high school and with the Black History Program. I feel that I won't take for granted the history of my ancestors and the leaders that struggled for me to have the rights that I have today.

Q. What do you feel that administrators need to know when implementing a Black History Program?

I would tell them first off that they can say things that might offend White people but it is not White History Month. It is Black History Month and as long as the speaker is telling the truth and getting a powerful message to the Black kids, let them say what it is they feel. If it is going to make a difference in just one kid's life, then say it regardless of who's watching.

Shelia has recently been married and hopes to work one day in the computer technology field. She sees this experience as one that has given her the will to accomplish despite the odds.

Sandra

Sandra is working at a doctor's office as a medical technician. She has immediate plans to enter a community college and pursue a business degree. Her goals are to one day own a business and to be an independent real estate agent who will give back to her community. Sandra said that her parents were illiterate and never finished school. As a child, most of her academic help came from her sisters, and her parents used their educational shortcomings as fuel for motivation. She recalled that her parents would always tell her that they wanted her to be "better than them."

Q. How do you remember the events associated with the Black History Program and Student Protest?

I remember it well and I remember the speaker. He spoke something about life and what we should look out for. And what should be taking place. And how we should go about life as it is today. And what to look out for exactly. I remember that some of the teachers were walking out and I remember that some of the White kids [were also walking out]. And I'm not a racial person, but I remember most of them checking out of school that day in fear that we were supposed to beat them up or something. And it was this one White student who stayed-her name, I shouldn't give her name. And I asked her why everybody was checking out and she said because they feared we were going to beat them up. Which I have no reason to beat nobody up. I am a peaceful person and, um, the media was very, very unfair. The media went about . . . I would say the media was supposed to be fair and they basically showed what they wanted to show. And the people who wanted to speak, they did not show at all. The people who spoke for the speaker, they edited them out, they didn't show them. That [next] day, I just knew the system was corrupted altogether. Here it was I was getting off the bus my defense is what has happened now. What did I do, it was like teachers were looking funny, everybody was in fear of something. And still half of the student body didn't show up and it was mainly Caucasian kids. And it was like, "What the heck is going on?" although I never asked any questions and I went on about my business. I had a feeling, because of the fact [that] all the white kids, all the Caucasian kids, were not there. I guess their parents maybe, or somebody, called them and told them somebody is going to beat up so-and-so.

Q. Which aspect of the Black History Program impacted you the most?

It was a part in there where [the speaker] came to . . . and I remember it well. And he went down to the different groups and talked about the NAACP, which is for colored people, he talked about the Ku Klux Klan, and he compared the two. The Ku Klux Klan which he did bring in there, which he was bringing out the cruelty in them. What they had done to a little pregnant girl who was eight months pregnant. How they had cut open her womb and the baby fell on the ground and he was speaking of the cruelty and he was saying that, um, you know, just basically be aware. And the media. I remember the media well; they put that on T.V. And the little guy who spoke about it, he was a Caucasian, [and] did not bring it out how the speaker brought it out at all.

Q. What motivated you to engage in protest?

Well, because they transferred a teacher whom I say had no reason to be transferred in the first place. This teacher, I thought—which, I was a part of the protest—the teacher brought insight about what I should look forward to in the future. The teacher had in the class guest speakers that came in and talked to us. They also spent time with us as a student body and felt that the teacher should not have been transferred. I was a part of the protest and the media did hear what I had to say.

Q. How has this experience impacted your life?

I know how to ask a whole bunch of questions when I need to because in the past, I used to just keep my mouth shut and just let certain people just run over me. And now today, people look at me like, "Let her do her thing, she knows what she is doing, she is well prepared." And the time before this experience, I used to be just hush and not look for certain things. Let's look- right now, there is a football player on trial for murder. I don't know who the women are, but I am watching this constantly on T.V. Like, you know, the O.J. Simpson trial, where he was accused of killing Nicole Brown. And I see more and more people are being incarcerated. As I look at this, I thought maybe I should become a lawyer because if you don't listen and you don't pay attention, you are in trouble. And that is mostly one of the things that I learned being in that teacher's class, and what the speaker was saying at the Black History Program [was that] if you don't pay attention, you are going to be left out.

I see myself more as a leader [now]. And being that I am a mother, I am trying to channel my kid's mind. That she should be a leader, because I was a follower once, it did not work. If you live your life for other people, you are not living your life at all. You live your life for you and that is all that matters.

Q. What do you feel school administrators need to know when implementing a Black History Program?

I would say to them, you find a good teacher that is going to influence young minds, because I was there. I was a student and the speaker influenced my mind better than anyone else at a Black History Program. In the other programs that were in the past, you could say that I was going to sleep, but this speaker spoke and I was up and awake. Find somebody that is going to motivate young minds instead of putting them to sleep.

Tony

Tony has completed a Bachelor's degree in English Education and plans to pursue a Master's degree in Education. His primary goal is to become a teacher at his former high school. He believes that he can bring significant changes to the school. As a child, Tony grew up with his grandmother; his parents' financial situation forced him into this position. His parents also divorced, and he was very saddened as a child that he did not have parents at home for the typical evening meals. He said they "were poor, but not as poor as I thought"; he remembers riding to the grocery store in a taxi, which was very embarrassing. However, Tony pointed out that unlike some kids who didn't have money for a taxi, his grandmother could at least pay for the service.

Q. How do you remember the events associated with the Black History Program and Student Protest?

Well, actually at that particular program, I remember that the students were actually interested in seeing what the minister would talk about. Because before, I remember that the Black History Programs that we had prior to this one weren't successful in the planning, there wasn't much interest in the guest speaker. Usually when you have a Black History Program, people are interested in knowing the person. Maybe to research to see if that person has any literature out or interviews so they can learn about that person. I remember I myself wanted to hear what this person had to say. I think the difference came into play when they found out who the person was, being a minister from the Nation of Islam. Because what people . . . people have stereotypes of people and I think that maybe some of the people were misinformed. They weren't educated enough to learn about everything. For instance, they may know one negative thing and they ran with it. I remember that particular guest speaker causing-I wouldn't say a controversy because of them being uneducated. People being uneducated. What made it different was the interest knowing that he had affiliation with the Nation of Islam and a lot of times they just tell you the way they see things. The just tell it like it is [and] they don't try to sugarcoat stuff or they will bring to the table some issues that people don't want to talk about that often. And I think that is what they were expecting- that he would bring to the program something that they maybe thought people weren't ready to hear or kids weren't grown up to hear.

I was confused [the day after the program]; I didn't know what for. I didn't know what was going on, I thought something had happened prior to me getting to school that morning. I thought maybe a fight had broken out when I first walked in the school. You usually see the assistant principal on duty and they weren't really saying anything. But you know, you go to your cliques, [and] when I finally made my way to the students that I usually hang out with, they were talking about the Black History Program. And how some parents had called the superintendent and principal that night, after the Black History Program. I assumed they thought that maybe a fight would break out or something. I can say myself personally that it was only Black students in class the next day because the White parents thought that fights would break out. I even remember being in the class with one particular white student. She was cool with everybody, she managed to get along with everybody both Black and White. And she mentioned that her parents told her she shouldn't go. But she knew nothing would happen. And she said, "No, I am going to school, I know these students. I know everyone and I attended the program, I didn't see anything wrong." She said she maybe would have reworded a few things, but she didn't take offense to them. We didn't go on with the scheduled lesson plans, we actually had a group discussion and some of the instructors led the discussion. We also had a lot of teachers absent and we actually sat and talked about it.

I think it is such a close-knit community-some of the parents may talk to teachers and they may attend the same church. I'm sure a teacher, if they are close friends, called parents and ministers. And when they talked they said, you know, they got the word out. If you have a speaker and you have thirty people in there, you are going to have thirty different versions of what that speaker said. So I'm sure what was said was left in different versions. I'm sure that had an effect on some of the teachers not being there. Because I remember one teacher being kind of cold to the students. I am sure if they didn't want to be there they could have taken one of their days off. Because you have so many days or maybe they were there just to see what was going to happen.

Q. How did the Black History Program impact your life? What did you learn?

I felt empowered because you saw someone who had taken a stand. He knew what he was talking about, he seems [sic] well educated. He had to be in order to present those facts. I felt as though I had learned something [and] I had gained something from the total experience. It made a good impression. And that goes back to the stereotypes of those students that I saw dressed up in suits and looking neat and presentable. It looked like they had on their Sunday's best. I wouldn't normally see them like that walking around school. And for them to be dressed up and ready for that program, it made others students, younger kids who looked up to them, were like, "If they can be presentable, I can also." It caught your attention-they were acting like young men that day, like more mature men. We realized that the reason we were fighting each other was because we were ignorant and we didn't want to learn from each other. Everyone of us could bring something to the table. And maybe what was going on in my home wasn't going on in somebody else's, but maybe [there was] something that I could learn from that. At one time we weren't seeing eye to eye, but with the help of that instructor, the teacher, we learned that we could get along, [and] because of that we became good friends. So we learned that being together we were very powerful. What one of us was lacking, the other made up for, so we realized that we could voice our opinion to the principal and the school board and we just had to suffer the repercussion. And what we believed was that we had something concrete.

Q. What motivated you to engage in protest and how did you feel while engaging in the protest?

The removal of the teacher was what sparked the protest. I can speak on my behalf, the teacher was very beneficial to me because he pushed me to do things in school that I probably would not have done, had I not been under his guidance. They wanted to remove that teacher and also there was the controversy when the principal was fired. I was a part of the protest and we were standing in front of the school board with flyers and the school board is on Main Street. They had people who were stopping. And many who joined in the protest. Some even went in to attend the meeting. I think at some point they closed the meeting because they had so many people. They were filled to capacity. There were a lot of people protesting outside. We were also protesting because there used to be fights between students and that teacher had actually brought students together. So we came together from different communities and actually began to appreciate the differences we had and so we decided to come together. And there were also parents. I remember meeting with a prominent Black figure in the community. The parents got together and discussed and some of the students got together. I remember myself being one of them. There were also White students protesting with us. . . . And also the teacher was well liked by all the students. And he made the hard heads listen. I remember I wrote an article about the protest and about 1/3 of the students were White.

I remember feeling good about the whole situation. I knew that I was standing up for a cause. I knew I had the support of my grandmother and other family members, my aunts and uncles, and even the pastor of the church. It was just good to see all those people there because I didn't feel like I was alone. I remember having the support of the priest and nun. We were happy to have the support of the White students. It showed that the speaker wasn't prejudiced if there were White students protesting.

Q. How has this experience impacted your life?

It made me realize a lot. It made me more open to listening to people and how they feel about Black History. A lot of the issues with the school are political. There is a lot of prejudice and when you see it and it is actually right up in your face, it is different.

Q. What, to you, is the importance of a Black History Program?

Recently at another school they were talking about not having a Black History Program, but just as at that school, we felt that Black History Program was needed. You notice in our American History books there are few Black people that are mentioned and they are scattered. Or they will talk more about slavery. And I know as an African American person that is not all we had as far as history. I think that it is very important to have Black History in the schools, because of what is left out of books. And what people don't include. Because it is not "necessary." But history is important for the Black student so they can feel a part of, not just about, slavery. I would become upset if Black History was not there. Because I would feel that we would be at a disadvantage, not being able to have Black History Programs in our schools. I think that it is a time when everyone can gain something and I think everyone gets something out of the programs, if they are structured right-both Black and White students and whatever other races you would have present.

Q. What do you feel school administrators need to know when implementing a Black History Program?

I would say that it is important to be familiar with the school; some people just want to recite poems. It is important to have a quality Black History Program. I guess I would be the thorn in their sides because I would be interested in putting together a Black History Program that has quality. I would also say that it is a waste of time to have students just sing songs for a Black History Program. Make it worthwhile for students.

Meeka

Meeka is currently working with children in a behavioral clinic. Meeka lived with her parents in Texas until the age of six; afterwards, she moved to Louisiana to live with her aunt and uncle. Prior to completing high school in

Louisiana, Meeka moved back to Texas and graduated from high school. Meeka plans to one day own a business. In the interview with Meeka, we were intrigued by her stamina to overcome personal obstacles that could have caused her to lose sight of her academic goals.

Q. How do you remember events associated with the Black History Program and Student Protest?

First of all, the controversy was uncalled for and some of the students took what was said out of context. They went home and told their parents. I really don't think it should have been handled to such an extreme because everybody was fine except a couple of students who took it too far.

When a lot of White people walked out of our Black History Program and we believed that if we sat and learned . . . it was true, teachers walked out first and some students followed. And we just felt that this wasn't right-we sit and learn White history in class and we don't walk out. We were learning something and we felt it was disrespect for them to walk out on our Black History Program.

Q. How did the Black History Program impact your life?

Well, this program was different from the traditional Black History Programs. You didn't get the regular traditional talk about Martin Luther King. The speaker talked about things that were going on in the United States, how Black people were; he was teaching us knowledge about ourselves, about what was going on around us. That we should open up our eyes and see what was going on and that was something different from traditional Black History Programs.

Q. What motivated you to engage in protest?

Well, when they transferred the teacher, they knew they were taking away something from the students. Because this teacher was a person that really understood the students and he took time out to sit and talk with us and they felt if they took this person away the school would be under control or something. The reason I took part was because I felt it was just plain wrong. Because this teacher taught us real Black History, he wasn't a person that just sat around and took anything. He didn't teach out of the book. He taught us about the world, he brought in the newspaper, he brought in things that were going on currently and that was the best thing for the students. And they took the best thing for the students away.

Q. How has this experience impacted your life?

Well, the way the protesting and all the things that happened affected me was that I learned that you don't have to just accept anything. I learned that if you get with a group of people that are commonly together on one thing, you can get something done. You don't have to sit around and accept what people give you. Take a stand and get things done. I mean, in my job I ran into a few situations where I was the person—being my age, going through what I have been through—am the person that took a stand and said "We can do better than this." A lot of the older people just didn't understand because they haven't been through what I have been through. It just made me not fear to take a stand. Cause I already have taken a stand before. If I take a stand, I can get something done.

Q.   What do you feel school administrators need to know when implementing a Black History Program?

I would let the school board know we are in a world of change. We need to get off of that traditional stuff. Our Black kids need to know some today history, the things that are going on today and things that are going on right around them. I would let them know that we need a Black History Program that is going to teach, instead of something that has already been taught. They need new information, that is what the students are looking for; they want to know something new. They don't want to hear the same old Martin Luther King and Harriet Tubman-that's old. We want something new and that is what a lot of kids are hungering for, that is why a lot of kids don't care about school. They are tired of that old stuff; they want something new. And every time something new comes in, they [administrators] want to kick it out.

Rhonda

Rhonda grew up in a single-parent home. She had one sibling, an older sister, who was primarily responsible for taking care of her. Rhonda specifically reflected on her mother having to work two jobs, which caused her to be absent from the family. Currently, Rhonda has a family of her own: two children and a husband. At the time of the study, she was pursuing a degree in elementary education. Rhonda hopes to work in a rural school district; preferably in the district she attended high school.

Q.   How do you remember events associated with the Black History Program and Student Protest?

It was very stressful, especially how the minority group handled the things. They weren't forced to attend the Black History Program and the White parents didn't want their children to interact with the program. For them not to be there was disrespectful. It is a part of history, and just the title "Black History" doesn't mean anything. It is actually a part of history. We did sit in class and learn about Abe Lincoln and Theodore Roosevelt and everybody else. But very seldom [did] we learn about our heritage.

Q. How did the Black History Program impact your life?

I felt good; I actually learned a lot of things because [the speaker] taught me a great deal about things that happened on the plantation. How they did pregnant women-I didn't know all of that; I was actually surprised it was like that. We usually learn about Martin Luther King and Rosa Parks and the Civil Rights Movement, but [other speakers] don't go in depth about how they were treated during that time. They stated a few statements, but what he gave was graphic, you could actually see or feel how our people felt. I know that through proper procedure, anything can be done. The Black History Program taught me not to let anyone get over one [on me]. But the protest, even though everything didn't work out the way we wanted, we still were heard. And it made it much easier for me to know that I spoke my mind, that someone actually listened.

Q. What motivated you to engage in protest?

Well, we were very organized-we got together and decided we weren't going to let the teacher be transferred. He had changed a lot of our lives, got a lot of students off of the street. And we didn't feel it was right to take his job away or move him, because he had done so much for our school. We were told that if we didn't go back to class, the police would take us away. I was involved because I felt he was a good teacher. And he was doing things on our behalf. He wasn't doing things to make himself look good; he cared about us, and he wanted us to have everything that we could have. Anything was possible; he wanted to make sure that when we got into the world, we were ready for it.

Q. How has this experience impacted your life?

It made me look at myself and how I treat others; and how others treat me; whether or not I'm being treated equal. I grew a lot after the program; it opened my eyes a lot.

When I am at work and I want something done, and I know it's supposed to be done in a certain way I say, "We have to do something about this." When management is not doing what they are supposed to be doing. And when we are doing our jobs, we do what they ask us to do and they are not doing what they are supposed to do. So I take a leadership position.

Q. What do you feel school administrators need to know when implementing a Black History Program?

If you put things in [that] students want to learn, they may learn things they do not want to learn because they know something is in the curriculum that they want. It would encourage them to do better in the classroom.

Jackie

Jackie was raised in a two-parent home and recalls that at the age of nine, her mother passed away. After the death of her mother, Jackie was raised by her father. Jackie also mentioned that she has been attending school in this district ever since her mother's death. At the time of the study, Jackie was enrolled in college and working.

Q. How do you remember events associated with the Black History Program and Student Protest?

The student body at Southern High has always had a Black History Program where every student is allowed to be in the gymnasium. However, this year they decided to split the program into three separate programs and that way not everyone would be together as a unified student body. In the first program that was held, the content was not exactly what the students expected. That included African American students and White American students. Whenever we put on a program in the past, it would be a program that would relate the past Black people to current Black people. And this program was not what students expected. Some students became angry about it at first, and then it turned into a protest. In the past, I myself and other students helped to put the program together. This program was put together by a committee of teachers and that caused a conflict. But when students were involved, then naturally we have a keen insight about what the students want. I was Student Council President, and I was aware that the program was going to be put on by a certain group of teachers; however, I was unaware that the students felt this strongly about it.

Q. How has this experience impacted your life?

I did learn that students can express themselves and it has helped me in a large way to realize that everything is important. It changed me to realize that you can stand up for something and get your point across. For example, we protested and things were changed. The situation was reevaluated and [the school] turned out to have a good program. I definitely learned that if you can protest in the right manner, you can have a good outcome.

Thematic Analysis

According to Miles and Huberman (1984), thematic analysis allows the collection and use of qualitative information in a manner that facilitates communication with a broader audience. Seidman (1998) states:

First I use profiles of individual participants and group them into categories that make sense. Second, I mark individual passages, group these in categories, and then study the categories for thematic connection within and among them. (p. 102)

Thematic analysis is important because it allows the researcher to use a variety of types of information in a substantial manner that increases the accuracy of sensibility in understanding and interpreting the transcribed interviews (Boyatzis, 1998; Dumbuya, 2000).

We used thematic analysis as a process to encode the qualitative information gathered during the interviewing process of the seven participants at a Louisiana high school. The various themes introduced in this sectioin represent patterns found in the information. These patterns describe and organize aspects of the phenomenon encountered in the interviews. This section outlines the themes as they emerged from each participant's point of view. These emergent themes frame the discussion in this section. To better understand the first theme that emerged, the next section will briefly discuss the controversy around Black History. This will be followed by the first theme, which explains the primary reason for the controversy at Central High School.

Table 1 depicts a condensed demographic chart with brief individual biographies that assisted us in subsequent thematic analysis. Four of the participants were college students, one attended technical school, and the other two had full-time jobs.

Table 1: Demographic Data of Student Leaders

Pseudonym	Age	Occupation
Janice	22	College Student
Shelia	21	Technical School Student
Sandra	26	Medical Technician
Tony	22	College Student
Meeka	21	Counselor
Rhonda	20	College Student
Jackie	18	College Student

Controversy

The controversy around the implementation of Black History into the curriculum has been an ongoing problem for educational institutions in the United States. There are currently proponents and opponents of the implementation of Black History into the curriculum. This controversy around Black History has often resulted in student protest, in which students have demanded the implementation of a relevant Black History curriculum.

In this study, the seven student leaders explain from their experiences reasons why the Black History Program at their school was a controversial issue. In narrative form, these student leaders explain the Black History Program and student protest. This section also identifies reasons why there was controversy around this Black History Program. In this chapter, the researchers discuss the six major themes resulting from the student interviews in the following order: misinformation, monocultural attitudes and racism, awareness, empowerment, teachers who care, and student voice in planning curriculum.

One of the primary reasons behind much of the controversy around Black History Programs is a result of misinformation. Since the curriculum of most educational institutions in America has been dominated by Eurocentric ideology, this has caused great controversy regarding the implementation of Black History Programs.

Traditionally, schools have very seldom mentioned the accomplishments, achievements, and the impact that people of African descent have had on world history. Any mention of history from the African-centered perspective is viewed as non-history. Schlesinger (1992) expresses this as the "corruption of history as history." Lefkowitz (1996) sees Black History, or Afro-centrism, as a way to teach mythology rather than history.

As a result, when Asante (1988), Karenga (2002), and Muhammad (1965) mention the history of people of African descent, this is met with hostility. The result has been controversy. In schools where Black History is taught from an Afrocentric view, the dominant culture and those in power seek to crush its presence. As Banks (2002) mentions, it is more likely that Sacajawea would be included in the curriculum because she helped Whites conquer Native peoples, whereas Geronimo would be excluded because he resisted White takeover of Native lands. This scenario is all too often played out during Black History Month.

Theme 1: Misinformation

A primary purpose of this research project was to determine the major factors that contributed to the controversy at Central High School. It is believed that by uncovering what caused the controversy, other schools and school districts planning to implement Black History Programs into the curriculum can become informed about problems that may occur. Through in-depth interviews with student leaders, a major cause of the controversy around this Black History Program was concluded to be the result of misinformation. Misinformation was a theme that emerged from examining the narrative experiences of student leaders. A deeper look at what we call misinformation can also be situated by what we would call propaganda. One of the ways that the Euro-centered curriculum has been able to maintain its presence is through propaganda. This propaganda usually plays to the fear of Black violence. At this Black History Program, the propaganda appealed to the idea that Black students would become violent. This played to the chorus of those who were already opposed to Black history, as it was already perceived by some White teachers and students as unnecessary. Banks (2002) calls these misconceptions, which are used to justify the need for the elimination of multicultural education. These misconceptions point to the idea that Black history and multicultural education is against the West.

The experiences narrated by these student leaders indicate that part of the controversy that followed the Black History Program was a result of misinformation. This misinformation led to the contingent of law enforcement and school administrators coming to the school the day after the Black History Program.

Some of the students also expressed the disrespect that White students have toward Black History Programs. The fact that a few teachers walked out of the program confirmed their disrespect for Black History. There was also a conflict about what was true and false. The students indicated that historical facts were distorted and the truth was something that not everyone wanted to hear. The major cause of the misinformation may have to do more with the fact that this program critically examined social issues that impact African Americans. In doing this, the program had attacked the myths of freedom and equality as the basis for American ideals. Pinar (2004) calls this an *official story:*

> The official story a nation or culture tells itself-often evident in school curriculum hides other truths. The national story also creates an illusion of truth being on the social surface, when it is nearly axiomatic that the stories we tell ourselves mask the unacceptable truths. What we as a nation try not remember-genocide, slavery, lynching, prison rape-structures the politics of our collective identification and imagined affiliation. (p. 38)

In an attempt to cover the pain that resulted in the unmasking of the official story, it became convenient to spread misinformation about the program.

Theme 2: Monocultural and Racist Attitudes

Monoculture is the idea that a concept should be viewed by only one cultural perspective. The idea of a monocultural attitude sometimes causes individuals to believe that their values, ideas, and concepts should be adopted by other ethnic groups. Monocultural attitudes often result in the disrespect of other peoples' ideas, concepts, history, and cultural values.

As we examined the narrative experiences of these student leaders, one of the themes that emerged was monocultural attitudes. Nieto (2004) describes the different levels of monocultural attitudes that seemed to prevail at this Black History Program:

> Racism is unacknowledged. Policies that support discrimination are left in place. These include low expectations and refusal to use students' natural resources in instruction. Only a sanitized and safe curriculum is in place. . . . All important knowledge is essentially European American. This Eurocentric view

is reflected throughout the curriculum, instructional strategies, and environment for learning. . . . Ethnic and/or women studies, if available, are only for students from that group. This is a frill that is not important for other students to know.

Compared with the students' stories, Nieto's points seem to be very accurate in describing the unacknowledged racism, a sanitized curriculum, and the monocultural attitudes displayed by White teachers and students. Student leaders particularly noted the disrespect teachers of Eurocentric backgrounds have for Black History. This disrespect was illuminated when some White teachers and students walked out of the Black History Program.

The student leaders seem to put stress on the fact that Black history is not perceived as being necessarily a part of history. This again coincides with the monocultural framework presented by Nieto where teachers and students feel that ethnic studies is "frill" that it is not important to know. The student leaders understood that this disrespect towards Black History seemed to be a result of the Eurocentric view that permeated the curriculum and the learning environment. Rhonda clearly points this out when she says, "*White* parents didn't want their children to interact with the program. We did sit in class and learn about Abe Lincoln and Theodore Roosevelt and everybody else [emphasis added]. But very seldom did we learn about our heritage." The monocultural attitudes present what Gary Howard (2006) describes in his book *We Can't Teach What We Don't Know*. The White teachers at this school seem to have been isolated from the history of oppressed groups in America. Thus, they were entrapped by the luxury of ignorance. In the book, Howard notes of his personal experiences:

> I realize that members of the dominant group in any society do not necessarily have to know anything about those people who are not like them. For our survival and the carrying on of the day to day activities of our lives, most White Americans do not have to engage in any meaningful personal connection with people who are different. This is not a luxury available to people who live outside of dominance and must, for their survival, understand the essential social nuances of those in power. The luxury of ignorance reinforces and perpetuates White isolation. (p. 12)

Howard's ideas about the luxury of ignorance seem to be a part of the problem related to the monocultural attitudes displayed by teachers and students. A more critical analysis of the situation reveals that racism was essentially at the core of the attitudes displayed at this Black History program.

Racism was at the core of this situation because the idea of White supremacy manifested itself when the White teachers walked out of the program. These teachers knew that they would not be reprimanded for this action. In conjunction with this, the White teachers knew they had the full backing of the majority of the school board administrators. This was demonstrated when a majority of White upper-level administrators visited the school the day after the program with sheriff deputies. The lynch mob had once again been conjured up with hopes of frightening the students, the community, and the teacher who organized the program. It didn't matter to these teachers and administrators that the school was majority African American. The bottom line was they didn't wish to see critical Black history, and they had the power to make sure that it was not implemented in schools. This equation is prejudice plus power-the key ingredients for racism.

Theme 3: Awareness

One of the reasons for the implementation of Black History Programs is that they create awareness about the history of people of African descent. Therefore, for African American children, the study of Black History is seen as a source of self understanding (Karenga, 2002). Karenga describes it best by saying that Black History is a reflection of people of African descent: who they are, what they can do, and equally important, what they can become as a result of the past which reveals their possibilities.

The Kawaida theory (Karenga, 2002) is a major factor in helping one gain awareness of self. The student leaders expressed that as a result of these experiences, they have become more aware of the social inequalities impacting their lives. Campbell (2004) notes that consciousness gives one awareness of the self and the environment. In analyzing their environment, students were able to locate the source of their oppression. Macedo (2000) brilliantly illustrates this point when he comments on Freire's work:

> Imagine that instead of writing Pedagogy of the Oppressed Freire had written Pedagogy of the Disenfranchised. The first title utilizes discourse that names the oppressor, whereas the second fails to do so. If you have an "oppressed," you must have an "oppressor" Pedagogy of the Disenfranchised dislodges the agent of the action while leaving doubt who bears the responsibility for such action. (p. 21)

This leaves the ground wide open for blaming the victim of disenfranchisement for his or her own disenfranchisement. As a result of this new consciousness, some White teachers feared that their attitudes, dispositions, and the role of White supremacy had been unveiled, thus causing them to seek some form of retribution on the students, the teacher who organized the program, and the principal. Some White teachers, administrators, and students also saw this as a threat to their dominant positions in the school.

A deeper analysis of the situation at this high school reveals that part of the problem was a direct result of the power relationship that existed prior to the Black history program. In this relationship, White teachers, administrators, and students walked out of Black history programs or either checked out of school without any reprimand from those in authority. This clearly demonstrated that because of their relationship with those in power, which was based on their race, they could do as they pleased without fear of being reprimanded. In addition,

Black history programs in the past had been largely presented from the perspective of the dominant group.

The earlier Black history programs offered what Banks (2002) calls the *contribution approach*, which is to simply celebrate and glorify the accomplishments of token African Americans. Nieto (2004) references this point when she points out how Dr. Martin Luther King has been historically engineered to fit the ideology of those in power. In this sense, the Black history programs of the past served the interests of those in the dominant group who wished to remain veiled in a manner that did not demonstrate their complicit racist attitudes.

More importantly, critical pedagogy, which helps one to uncover the role of power relations and how those relations can be uprooted, was never examined in previous Black history programs. Freire (2000) points out that it is only when the oppressed come to the realization that the oppressor has been internalized into their consciousness that the road to liberation can begin. In this study, the Black history program served to raise the consciousness of the students which caused "these formerly passive students to turn against their domestication and the attempt to domesticate reality" (p. 75). These students demonstrate the power of reflection and action, a praxis which can lead to a more humanizing society.

The student leaders saw this experience as something that made them more aware of their lived realities. It gave them the ability to understand how past events have shaped the current circumstances they face in their everyday lives. What the student leaders expressed coincides with Karenga's Kawaida theory. It should also be noted that this experience helped students to see life from an Afrocentric view as espoused by Asante (1988). Vann and Kunjufu (1993), in their analysis of how Columbus is taught in most schools, make reference to how the current curriculum has a Eurocentric value system. This experience for students also coincided with Kincheloe and Steinberg (1997), who noted that critical theory is a straightforward technique and does not sugarcoat the realities of the African American experience. Since the program, according to the students, was one that interested them and did not sugarcoat historical facts, they became aware of the persistent racism and oppression that pervade educational institutions and the larger society. This coincides with Freire's (2000) argument that "It is only when the oppressed find the oppressor out and become involved in the organized struggle for their liberation that they begin to believe in themselves" (p. 65). Student leaders in this situation began to take action after realizing the unjust practices that were being adjucated upon them. They began to understand that education is not a love for death but a love for life, and in this process they are transformative creative beings. In Freire's words,

> It is as transforming creative beings that humans in their permanent relations with reality, produce not only material goods-tangible objects- but also social institutions, ideas, and concepts. Through their continuing praxis, men and women simultaneously create history and become historical-social beings. (p. 101)

Thus this new awareness thus paved the way for student leaders to become empowered.

Theme 4: Empowerment

In examining power relationships and how they intersect with education, critical pedagogy can be used to examine the issues around the controversial Black History in this study. One of the questions that critical theory seeks to examine is, "Whose knowledge and for what purpose?" Historically, the education of African Americans has been designed by what Watkins (2001) calls "The White architects of Black education" for the purpose of control. Watkins notes the following about education: "Organized education, much like religion, has been long influenced by the forces of the power structure, the state and those with an ideological agenda" (p. 10).Woodson (1999) makes a similar observation when he points out that "The education of the Negroes, then, the most important thing in the uplift of Negroes, is almost entirely in the hands of those who enslaved them and now segregate them" (p. 24).

These points prove valid in contemporary times as African Americans do not have the power to determine what they believe their children should know. This was clearly demonstrated in the controversy around this Black History program, as the program was designed by students whereby the speaker demonstrated the power relationships that existed in the larger society and how this impacted African American people. Despite the program's success among the majority of students, it was considered problematic by those in power positions. Ultimately, what the speaker and social studies teacher had done was create a dialectical dialogue with the students. McLaren (2003) summarizes what happened at this Black history program when he says, "The purpose of dialectal educational theory, then, is to provide students with a model that permits them to examine the underlying political, social, and economic foundations of the larger White supremacist capitalist society" (p. 195). This dialectical discourse with students resulted in an unveiling of racism both in the school and in the larger society. In addition, the speaker and the social studies teacher raised the consciousness of students so that they could locate themselves. Kincheloe and Steinberg (1997) note that critical pedagogy is important in improving the lives of oppressed people. The student leaders explained how this experience empowered them by giving them a sense of pride and determination.

Another theory often associated with the critical theory is the *critical incident theory*. The critical incident theory explains how an incident can impact the way people view the world. It shapes their behavior and attitudes about certain issues. The school controversy and student protest centered on this Black History Program has empowered the student activists and helped shape how they see themselves and the world. It has given them a belief that they can accomplish whatever they desire. They also feel that this experience brought out their leadership characteristics.

One of the main goals of education is to bring out the gifts and talents that exist within people. This experience has empowered these former students in their everyday lives, helping them to realize the power and beauty of human potential.

Theme 5: Teachers Who Care

It has been well documented that teachers have a dramatic effect on student learning outcomes. When teachers are cognizant of their students' backgrounds, this is an important step in effectively teaching. The student protest at Central High School was the result of the transfer of a teacher. Students protested when the teacher who motivated them to achieve their educational goals was transferred from their school.

This protest by the students illustrates that young people want to learn. It also illustrates that they want to change the negative realities of their condition. More importantly, students made a special point about the importance of having teachers who really care about them. Gay (2000) notes that caring is manifested "in the form of teacher attitudes, expectations, and behaviors about students' human value, intellectual capability, and performance responsibilities" (p. 45). Throughout the interviews, what continued to emerge was that caring teachers "empower students by legitimizing their voice and visibility" (p. 49). Gollnick and Chinn (2006) describe the characteristics of caring teachers:

> They are patient, persistent, and supportive of students. They listen to students and validate their culture. They empower their students to engage in their education. Caring teachers don't give up on their students. They understand why students may not feel well on some days or are having a difficult time outside of school. Nevertheless, these teachers do not accept failure. (p. 366)

The student leaders' reflections about their teacher demonstrate that teachers do have the power to help change the reality of students. It should be highlighted that as the students mentioned, knowledgeable and caring teachers are needed to help students achieve their educational goals.

Theme 6: Voice in School Curriculum

The curriculum for most school districts in the U.S. has not changed dramatically. While there have been some changes, very few schools have allowed students the opportunity to have a voice in the curriculum. Gollnick and Chinn (2006) point out that:

Most schools today legitimate only the voice of the dominant culture—the standard English and world perspective of the white middle class. Many of the students, especially those from oppressed groups, learn to be silent or disruptive, and /or they drop out, in part because their voices are not accepted as legitimate in the classroom. (p. 368)

This has caused students to disregard many of the curricular activities implemented within the schools. The student leaders narrated that the traditional Black History Programs did not allow students to have a voice. The students thought that having a voice in this Black History Program created a desired learning opportunity. The students' interest and participation illustrated this, since this Black History Program was not consistent with traditional Black History Programs. Some students also expressed what they wanted policy makers to know about the implementation of Black History Programs. McLaren (2003) makes a special point in his book about the importance of student experiences and voices being a starting point in the educational process. In McLaren's words, "A student voice is not a reflection of the world as much as it is a constitutive force that both mediates and shapes reality within historically constructed practices and relations shaped by the rule of capital" (p. 245). The student leaders in this study verified that voice was an important aspect of the teaching and learning process (Gay, 2000; McLaren, 2003). When questioned about what they thought administrators should consider in the implementation of the Black History Programs and curricula, their thoughts coincided with the decision-making/social action approach espoused by James Banks (2005). Their thoughts also mirrored what Freire (2000) calls praxis, which is critical reflection, and action.

The student leaders narrated that one of the primary reasons for problems associated with this Black History Program was the lack of student input regarding the teacher transfer. Student leaders felt that administrators and board members should have been more cognizant of their voice. When administrators and school board members try to dismiss student needs and demands, the result is student protest. More importantly, the student responses mirrored what many in the field of multicultural education have noted in their research regarding controversial issues-in particular, those issues that might be seen as threatening to White dominance (Banks, 2002; Nieto, 2004). Too often, the more controversial issues with regard to race, class, and gender bias are often dismissed in an attempt to make students believe that we live in a colorblind society. Marshall (2002) points out that the assumption of racelessness may do more harm than good for students because it may result in internal and psychological problems for African American students. Teachers and administrators often assume that school is neutral. However, Freire (2000) points out that education is never neutral, it is political; the mere act of teaching is political.

We have come to understand through this interview process the need for student voice when implementing a curriculum. If anything, the students want to be stakeholders in their educational process. Having a voice "suggests the means that students have at their disposal to make themselves heard and to define themselves as active participants in the world" (McLaren, 2003, p. 245.) Student leaders' demand for a voice in the curriculum process is not something new; these leaders were saying in essence that "human existence cannot be silent, nor can it be nourished by false words, but only in true words, with which men and women transform the world" (Freire, 2000, p. 88).

Chapter 6

Conclusion

The purpose of this study was to find out about the narrative experience of student activists with regard to a Black History Program and student protest in a southern high school. A qualitative study was used to conduct this research. Since we wanted to discover how the student activists experienced this phenomenon, a phenomenological study was used. We used an in-depth interview technique to gather the data. This chapter presents a discussion of the findings, the implications of the study, recommendations for school districts, school administrators, parents, and students. This chapter concludes with concluding remarks regarding the struggle for Black history.

Discussion of Findings
Critical Pedagogy

The term *critical pedagogy* has roots in both the Frankfurt school of thought and the early ideas of Black leaders, scholars, and activists. This theory addresses issues about improving the lives of oppressed people (Kincheloe & Steinberg, 1997). Freire (2000), while working with oppressed minority groups, used the term to describe relationships and discourse used to empower minority students. Critical pedagogy is a straightforward approach to teaching; it does not lend itself to sugarcoating or watering down the realities of everyday life for minority people. Critical pedagogy is seen as a way to empower students.

This study found that critical pedagogy empowers minority youth. At Central High, the difference between this Black History Program and the previous Black History Programs was that the speaker used critical pedagogy. The students indicated that the speaker did not sugarcoat the realities of history. One student even said that the speaker brought to the table some issues that most people were afraid to confront. Students also mentioned that critical pedagogy was used by one of their teachers. A student indicated that the teacher brought in newspapers and current events; another student talked about the teacher bringing in guest speakers, and more importantly, how the teacher linked these events to issues of power.

Events associated with the Black History Program and student protest have given the student activists a sense of empowerment. Student activists indicated that they felt empowered; all of these events have given student activists the determination to strive for achievement. They also indicated that they became more outspoken—initially, the students indicated that they would not speak out about certain issues. The sense of empowerment has carried over to the every-day lives of the student activist. Some indicated that when they are on the job and something happens that is contrary to what they believe, they speak out against it. Perhaps one of the greatest things that student activists gained from this experience is the knowledge that there is power in unity. When people are united for a common cause, they can voice their opinions in a peaceful manner.

For one student activist, the sense of empowerment was that the student protest transcended race.

Critical Black Pedagogy in Education

Critical pedagogy has been summed up as an analysis of the relationship between power and knowledge (McLaren, 2003). The analysis of power and knowledge has included numerous African American leaders, African American scholars, African American educators, and others involved in the struggle for equality and freedom of African Americans. Some of the earliest ideas about critical pedagogy emerged when Carter G. Woodson (1999) expanded the idea about the need for Black history. Woodson eloquently argued that "the education of the Negroes, then the most important thing in the uplift of the Negro, is almost entirely in the hands of those who have enslaved them and now segregate them" (p. 22). Woodson further examined this relationship between power and knowledge: "the thought of the inferiority of the Negro is drilled into him in almost every class he enters and almost every textbook he studies" (p. 2). The essential problem with Central High's Black History Program was the fact that White people still had control over the education of the masses of African Americans. While the Black History Program and the African American Studies course at this school proved to be instrumental in motivating students, ending student resistance, and making students conscious, this was viewed as disruptive by the majority of the White school board members. The contemporary problems of this Black History Program with regards to White power and control of Black thought were clearly articulated by several African American leaders, scholars, and activists.

Elijah Muhammad, a most powerful figure in American and world history, articulated the ideas of critical pedagogy in a very profound way. Muhammad (1965) pointed out the following:

> Certainly the so-called Negroes are being schooled, but is this education the equal of that of their slave-masters? No; the so-called Negroes are still begging for equal education. After blinding them to the knowledge of self and their own kind for 400 years, the slave masters refuse to civilize the so-called Negroes into the knowledge of themselves of which they were robbed. The slave-masters also persecute and hinder anyone who tries to perform this rightful duty. (pp. 44 -45)

Elijah Muhammad correctly describes the historical and contemporary problem facing African American students. Despite the positive impact of the Black History Program on African American children, it was seen as threatening. Elijah Muhammad brilliantly points out that anyone who performs this great task of awakening the Black mind will be persecuted. The issues around Central's Black History Program and curriculum demonstrate the validity of Muhammad's words. Muhammad further explains that to be rulers over rulers you will need superior knowledge. The great fear of the awakening of the Black mind, or as Elijah Muhammad calls it, "the resurrection," is threatening to those who rule. Elijah Muhammad proposed and brought knowledge that was necessary for the resurrection of the Black mind. Muhammad pointed out that the knowledge of God and self were two necessary components in the awakening of the Black mind. Those who make the educational decisions realize this most important truth regarding self knowledge and have purposely maintained a curriculum and ideology that reinforced their ideas.

Watkins (2005) points that "While resistance is inevitable, the dominant ideas of any society are the ideas of its ruling class" (p. 111). This is why certain forms of knowledge must be kept away from the people. If the people were given the right kind of knowledge, they would be free from the control of the ruling class. Black history happens to be one of those bodies of knowledge that has remained hidden from the masses, but in particular African Americans.

Marcus Garvey, like Woodson and Muhammad, asked questions regarding Black education: Where is the Black man's flag? Where is his nation? Where is his army? These questions stimulated Garvey's desire to set up a government for African Americans. Garvey understood that in setting up government, education would be a central component; he therefore urged African Americans to "know" themselves. Garvey's ideas were similar to those of Elijah Muhammad, who stated that African Americans needed an educational system that they could call their own. The controversy at Central High School highlights the importance of having an independent Black educational system. The struggle for Black history continues even after we have entered the new millennium.

Critical Race Theory

Critical race theory (CRT) and critical White studies are two fields of study that have emerged to inform our understanding of education. Critical race theory is primarily concerned with the connections between race and its impact on American life. Billings (2003) notes the origin of critical race theory: "Critical race theory sprang up in the mid-1970s with the early work of legal scholar Derrick Bell and Alan Freeman, both whom were distressed over the slow pace of racial reform in the United States" (p. 8).

Critical race theory considers racism to be a normal part of American life. More importantly, critical race theorists seek to expose racism and its impact on American life.

Critical race theory could be used to analyze the controversy around Central's Black History Program and curricula. Gollnick & Chinn (2006) point out, "critical race theory also focuses on racism in challenging racial oppression, racial inequities, and white privilege" (p. 11). Stovall (2005) identifies two major aspects of critical race theory as educational protest and scholarship. More importantly, Stovall links critical race theory to identification of White supremacy in education and methods used to eradicate its dominance in education.

Critical race theory, in the context of this research, is linked together in several ways. One of the major underpinnings of this study as described in both the case study and student interviews was the role of racism, privilege, and White supremacy. In the case study, concerned parents pointed out that "racism was and is the basis used in past historical events that caused races to be intimidated and deprived of human dignity." The head of the NAACP also discussed the institutional role of racism in this Louisiana school district. He noted how the schools system was racist for allowing White teachers to walk out of Black history programs. The students also pointed out the monocultural and racist attitudes displayed by some teachers and students. The disrespect toward Black history was seen as disrespect toward African Americans.

Another component of CRT examines White privilege, which was clearly observed as we examined the case study and student narratives. This privilege was manifested as some teachers who walked out of the program did so knowing they would not be reprimanded. Walking out of Black History programs had been an ongoing phenomenon prior to this particular Black History Program. White privilege was illuminated when White school administrators showed up the day after the program with sheriff deputies. The show of force has been attributed to one teacher who phoned the school board indicating there would be violence at the school. The privilege of having White skin afforded these teachers with a level of comfort that paved the way for them to openly display their racist attitudes. In fact, one teacher had the audacity to tell the African American students he felt bad for them because they had to hear another African American talk like that. Perhaps more insulting and illuminating was the apology by the school principal. The principal was forced by the Whites in power to hold an assembly apologizing for the Black History Program. This apology crystallized the racism, power, and privilege afforded to those in the dominant group.

As pointed out earlier, CRT is also concerned with educational protest. The student narratives clearly demonstrated this aspect. Immediately after the teacher who challenged White supremacy and the Euro-centered curriculum was transferred, parents and students protested. The parents formed a group called Concerned Parents Organization. This organization challenged the practice of racism at their school. In a letter to the local newspaper, the parents pointed out, "We have some racist teachers in our public schools, those who send their children to private schools." The parents in this study were in the forefront of identifying and challenging the unjust and inequitable school policies in this school district.

The students were also very active in this challenge. The students displayed their anger by walking out of school for several days. In addition to this, they attended several school board meetings to protest the decisions at their school. The student protest demonstrated a newfound consciousness of the individual and institutional racism. While on the surface the student protest seemed to be primarily centered on the teacher at this school, deeper analysis suggests that the student protest had implications beyond the teacher. The students were in fact protesting against a system that had sought to reduce them to beings for others. They had come to the realization of what Freire (2000) called "domestication" and Woodson (1999) called "mis-education." The students realized the teacher's role in awakening and inspiring them to become committed and re-educated, which instilled in them a sense of hope and purpose. They had come to believe that they had value and others had value, which could be used to create an atmosphere of love. However, the students saw in the transfer of their teacher the contradiction of education. As a result, "these contradictions [led] formerly passive students to turn against their domestication and the attempt to domesticate reality" (Freire, 2000, p. 75).

Kawaida Theory

Karenga (2002), an African American scholar, developed the Kawaida theory. Karenga believes that history is important in helping African Americans to understand present and future possibilities. Essentially, Kawaida theory is designed to help African Americans get a better understanding of who they are in the context of history. Kawaida theory, according to Karenga, will help African Americans develop a true self-concept.

Research findings indicate that Kawaida theory is important in helping students understand how past events have shaped current conditions. Student activists mentioned how they became cognizant of past events and how those events have shaped their current circumstances. One student mentioned that the speaker at this Black History Program noted that the obstacles confronting African

Americans today were shaped by past events. Another student indicated that the speaker was teaching African Americans knowledge about "ourselves."

Controversy around Black History

When Carter G. Woodson implemented the study of Negro History Week in 1926, his idea was met with hostility. What followed was a debate about the value of Black History for African American children. Opponents argued that Negro History Week would divide the country. It was also believed that Black History would result in the teaching of race, to which children should not be exposed. Finally, opponents of Black History argued that this type of education would be harmful to African American children.

Woodson argued that Black History would not divide the country, as it was already divided. Black History, according to Woodson, would serve the purpose of helping African Americans understand themselves. It would further help African Americans to become educated so they could do for themselves. Woodson thought that children should be taught Black History as they were confronted with the race problem every day.

What has followed several years after Carter G. Woodson's idea of Negro History Week is the debate about Black History and Multicultural Education. Opponents of Black History and Multicultural Education have mentioned that teaching Black History is more mythology than concrete history. Another recent argument is that Black history will result in the corruption of history. Furthermore, it is argued that this will result in the self ghettoization of African Americans.

One of the primary reasons of this research project was to examine the controversy that existed as a result of a Black History Program as possible means for debunking what opponents of Black History have put forth as an argument. Research findings from this study indicate that this program enlightened students. The emergent themes of awareness and empowerment illustrate this point. The student activists indicated that they became more aware of racial oppression. Students indicated that by becoming aware of the racial oppression experienced, they were better able to understand the circumstances that existed in their everyday lives. Contrary to opponents of Black History, none of the students indicated that Black History encouraged them to take a monocultural attitude toward other ethnic groups. And all of the students indicated that Black History empowered them in some way. The students said they gained self-respect, unity, and developed leadership characteristics. One student even indicated that her grades began to improve. The research findings from this study indicate that Black History is important in the education of African American youth.

Demands of Student Activists

The literature review noted two major demands of student activists; relevant classroom instruction and teachers who care. Kula (1969) concluded that student activists want a curriculum that is relevant. This relevant curriculum is action-oriented and allows students to participate in current social issues. In sum, this means that the student activists want a voice in the school curriculum.

Rosenthal and Jacobson (1967) found that students want teachers who care and have high expectations of them. This contributes to the self-fulfilling prophecy in students. Recent literature in multicultural education highlights the need for teachers who care, teachers with high expectations, and student voice as key components to an effective education program (Gay, 2000; Nieto, 2004; Gollnick, 2006). Research findings from this study indicated that students want a voice in the school curriculum and teachers who care about them. These were important factors that contributed to the student protest.

Some of the students indicated that this Black History Program was different because students were more involved with the planning. A student activist from another school indicated that the protest at her school was a result of students not being involved with the planning of the Black History Program. When the students protested for a different type of Black History Program, administrators then allowed students to make decisions about the type of Black History Program to be implemented. This resulted in a short protest and was followed by a successful Black History Program. In conclusion, student activists gave suggestions for school districts and administrators planning to implement Black History Programs into the curriculum. In their own voices, students indicated that a relationship between students and school administrators is important.

The cause of the student protest at Central High School was a result of the transfer of the teacher who organized the Black History Program. Student activists indicated that this teacher had helped them to attain many of their educational goals. Furthermore, the teacher cared about them and helped them to understand each other. The student activists protested when the teacher they felt had made significant changes in their lives was transferred. A student noted that this protest, which occurred a year after the Black History Program, had both Black and White student activists. This demonstrated, according to the students, that all students want teachers who care about them. Other students mentioned that the transfer of this teacher disturbed them. One student noted that many students dropped out of school as a result of the teacher being transferred. In the final analysis, students want teachers who care about them.

Implications of the Study

This study has given us insight into the problems that exist around the implementation of Black History Programs into the curriculum. The study provided information about the reasons for the controversy that surround Black

History Programs. It also described how student activists felt about the administrative changes that took place in a southern high school. We are confident that the information from this study could help school districts and school administrators planning to implement Black History Programs into the curriculum.

By being cognizant of the issues around the implementation of Black History Programs into the curriculum, school districts and school administrators can have insight about how to make Black History Programs a rewarding experience for all students. This will hopefully put to rest many of the myths and misconceptions about the value and purpose of Black History Programs. This study used detailed narrative information to support its interpretation process. It is believed that this can serve as a detailed, dynamic compliment to other studies.

In another context, it is hoped that this study will give insight about student activism with regard to Black History Programs. It could further serve the purpose of examining the impact of a relevant Black History curriculum on the attitudes and achievement level of African American students. The study adds to the literature information about high school student protest and its impact on student activists.

Recommendations

This study included the narrative experiences of student activists regarding a Black History Program and student protest in a Southern high school. In the section that follows we make recommendations for the following groups: school districts, school administrators, parents, and students.

Recommendations for School Districts

The following are recommendations for school districts planning to implement Black History Programs into the curriculum. School districts should: 1) develop a policy, 2) require Black History and Multicultural workshops for staff, and 3) initiate district-wide Black History Programs.

A policy should be developed by school districts outlining rules and regulations to be followed by schools when implementing Black History Programs into the curriculum. The rules should not include whom to invite as guest speakers or what type of program to implement. The rules should simply enforce the implementation of Black History Programs and outline time periods when activities should occur. One reason there is a disinterest in Black History Programs is that they are often held during the last period of the school day. This suggests that Black History Programs are not important.

Secondly, school districts should have Black History and Multicultural Education workshops. This should begin with school board members and administrators since they ultimately will make decisions regarding the implementation of Black History and Multicultural Education into the curriculum. This process will be very difficult, as it will require board members and administrators to literally be re-taught the history of African Americans and other oppressed groups, which will hopefully replace the Eurocentric dominance in education. We realize that this process for board members and administrators is equivalent to a robber who then gives the victim directions to the nearest police station. However, there should be forces in place to demand board members to participate in these training workshops. School districts should also require all district faculty to attend Black History and Multicultural Education sessions. These sessions should be provided to all employees before the start of the new school year, and should include a variety of Black History, Multicultural Education specialists. School districts can determine specialists by having community-based discussions and following prominent African American leadership.

Finally, school districts should implement district-wide Black History Programs. The district-wide Black History Programs would foster a greater appreciation for Black History. These events should be rotated to various schools within the school districts. We believe that this would foster better relationships between various schools and communities. Students would not see themselves as rivals but as unified peoples and communities. It should be noted that when we suggest unified peoples and communities, this is not limited to African Americans. Imagine a unified student populace transcending race, class, ethnicity, all working for a more equitable society.

Recommendations for School Administrators

This section provides recommendations for school administrators planning to implement Black History Programs into the school curriculum. School administrators should: 1) establish a school policy, 2) provide multicultural staff development education, 3) promote student dialogue, 4) confer with students, and 5) plan Black History Programs in advance.

Administrators should establish a school policy with regard to the implementation of Black History Programs. The policy should begin with a mission statement from school administrators. It should then be followed by a plan of action that gives instructions about the implementation of Black History Programs.

Secondly, school districts should provide additional Black History and Multicultural Education for staff. The Black History and Multicultural Education for staff development would reinforce the district-wide education plan. Whereas the district plan may require teachers to meet two to three days prior to the opening of school, the school plan could require meetings once a month.

Thirdly, school administrators should set times when students can have dialogue about issues regarding Black History and Multicultural Education. The purpose of dialogue is that it would prepare students for upcoming activities. It also helps students to value diversity among people. Periods of dialogue do not have to interfere with the regular school day. These periods can be held in homeroom before school starts or during the morning activity schedules. Finally, dialogue would give students the opportunity to discuss the type of Black History Program they would like.

Fourthly, school administrators should confer with students and student advisors to ascertain their ideas about the implementation of Black History Programs. The students indicated that administrators should listen to student concerns. As the students stated, the school is there to provide a service for them, and it is not entirely up to school administrators to decide the type of program that is implemented for a particular school year. One of the themes that emerged from the study was student voice and caring. When administrators listen to students, it portrays to students that administrators care about student needs. It is important to note that when students were involved with the implementation of the Black History Program, they were more attentive. When students do not have a stake in Black History Programs, they protest in a variety of ways. It is therefore important for school administrators to confer with students and their advisors.

Finally, Black History Programs should not be planned at the last minute. Black History Programs should be planned well in advance of the date that they are going to take place. Careful planning allows for individual creativity to be perfected in preparation for the program. The Black History Program at Central High School was carefully planned and this impressed upon the students its importance. Students expressed that they were attentive because they saw young men dressed in suits and ties. Planning is an essential part of making Black History Programs a success.

Recommendations for Parents

This section provides recommendations for parents when implementing Black History/Multicultural programs into the curriculum. Parents should: 1) develop a strong Parent Teacher Organization, 2) become politically active and 3) get involved with their children's education.

Parents should develop a strong Parent Teacher Organization. This organization should develop a mission statement that pertains to Black History. Of course, there may be parents who do not see the need for Black History Programs; however, this is why it is important for Parent Teacher Organizations to seek ways to provide educational training for parents. This awareness will hopefully dispel many of the myths and misconceptions that many parents were taught in school. Parent Teacher Organizations must seek some way to reach a consensus about this issue of Black history curriculum implementation. If consensus cannot be reached, then parents who wish to see Black History Programs implemented into the curriculum should develop an independent organization that promotes the study of Black History. This study has indicated that Black History can impact student attitudes about themselves. Therefore, it is imperative that parents push to see its implementation into the curriculum.

Parents must become politically active throughout their communities. They must form a force within the district that can have school board members voted out of office when their demands are not met. This will require economic resources that can be provided by civic organizations such as churches, businesses, etc. Parents should meet with individuals aspiring to be board members and require them to participate in Multicultural Educational workshops once elected. They should also inquire about the prospective school board candidate's views on Black History/Multicultural Education.

It is important for parents to get involved with their children's education. Many of the students indicated that a teacher at the school would constantly use racial remarks when referring to African American children. This should have been stopped when it first began; however, because parents were not involved with their children's education, it resulted in a student being expelled from school. Schools are supposed to nurture the gifts and talents of students. However, for African Americans, school has been a destructive force to their aspirations to achieve. Parents must not sit by and continue to let their children be subjugated to false ideas and concepts. Until parents become active in their children's education, those in power will continue to enforce a Eurocentric curriculum.

Recommendations for Students

This section lists recommendations for students when implementing Black History Programs into the curriculum. Students should: 1) develop a strong student government association, 2) continue to demand a voice, and 3) be prepared to protest.

Students should develop a strong student government organization. A strong student organization will be able to voice the demands of students. The student government association should work to see that students have a voice in the implementation of Black History Programs. The link between administrators, teachers, and students is the student government association. Furthermore, a strong student government association will be capable of mobilizing students and parents with regard to the implementation of Black History Programs.

Students should continue to demand a voice in the planning of relevant curriculum. As one student indicated, not all school board members, school administrators, and teachers are concerned with making African American students better individuals. If students continue to push for Black History Programs, administrators will be forced to listen to these demands. Student voices are important; it is like going to the doctor and not being capable of telling him what ails you. The patient must tell the doctor what ails him or her in order for the doctor to suggest a possible cure. In the same manner, students should voice their ideas and concerns.

Finally, students should be prepared to protest. One of the greatest aspects of the American society is the right to protest for rights. Students should familiarize themselves with peaceful protest tactics that may be necessary to use when school districts, administrators, and teachers seek to oppress them. Schools have recently witnessed new forms of student protest where students have begun to shoot teachers and fellow schoolmates. It is suggested that students should use Banks' (2002) social action approach to solving problems. This would require students to get involved with activities that will "allow them to take personal, social, and civic actions related to the concepts, problems, issues that they have studied" (p. 32). Students should remember that the school is their servant and they should use the school to gain valuable life experiences.

Concluding Remarks

We interviewed student activists about their experiences of a Black History Program and student protest. A modified Seidman (1998) interview technique provided the data needed to complete this study. This research began as a case study, and for the completion of this book, it evolved into a phenomenological study. An in-depth interview technique provided us with the opportunity to gain valuable information from the participants. Despite the small number of participants, their experience provided us with an abundance of information.

Finally, the great controversy over Black History implementation into the curriculum is something we feel should not even be debatable. Opponents of Black History implementation have not provided any information that proves that Black History is not good for African American children or any children for that matter. How many of the opponents of Black History have ever taught African American children? Research findings have continued to suggest that Black History can impact student attitudes and achievement. It is our aspiration to continue in the struggle for the implementation of Black History into school curriculum. We conclude this book with the words of Myrlie Evers Williams (2003), who captures the struggle for Black history and the role of education in transmitting this knowledge:

> It is impossible to develop future leaders of tomorrow without providing them with a solid historical foundation. When it is time to pass the torch, our youth must be ready. They must be armed with the tools that will help them forge the elements of tolerance and forgiveness into a universal shield of peace. It is imperative that they be equipped to ward off new attacks of hatred and discrimination. We provide these tools through education. (p. 7)

The struggle continues!

Bibliography

Alexander, C. (1982). The frequency and types of African American history month celebration programs in Chesapeake school system between 1980-1982. (ERIC Docu-
ment Reproduction Service No. 220355).

Akbar, N. (1998). *Know thy self.* Tallahassee, FL: Mind Productions.

Anyon, J. (1981). Social class and the hidden curriculum of work. *Curriculum Inquiry.*
11(81): p. 27.

Asante, M.K. (1988). *Afrocentricity.* Trenton, NJ: African World Press.

Asante, M. K. (1991). The Afrocentric idea in education. *Journal of Negro Education,* 60
(2), pp. 170-180.

Astin, A. (1970). Determinants of student activist. In J. Foster and D. Long. *Protest!
Student activism in America.* New York: William and Morrow.

Baker, H. (1993). *Rap: Black studies and the academy.* Chicago: University of Chicago
Press.

Banks, J. (2002). *An introduction to multicultural education* (3rd ed.). Boston: Allyn and
Bacon.

Banks, J. (2005). Multicultural education: Historical development, dimensions and practice. In J. Banks and C. Banks. *Handbook of research on multicultural education*
(2nd ed). New York: Macmillan Publishing.

Banks, J. & Grambs, J. (1972). *Black self concept.* New York: McGraw-Hill.

Banning, J. & McKinley, D. (1980). Conceptions of the campus environment. In J.H.
Morril and G. Oeeting (Eds.). *Dimensions of intervention of student development.*
New York: Wiley & Sons.

Barker, R.G. (1968). *Ecological psychology: Concepts and method for studying the environment of human behavior.* Stanford: Stanford University Press.

Bartley, M. (1973). Southern University student activism 1960-1963. M.A. Thesis:
Southern University, Baton Rouge, LA.

Bennett, W.J. (1992). *The de-valuing of America: The fight for our children.* New York:
Summit Books.

Bernal, M. (1996). The Afrocentric interpretation of history: Bernal replies to Lefkowitz.
Journal of Blacks in Higher Education, pp. 86-94.

Billings, G. (2003). *Critical race theory perspectives on social studies: The
profession, policies, and curriculum.* Greenwich, CT. Information Age Publishing.

Black history program sparks protest. (2000 February 24). *Baton Rouge Advocate.*

Board office picketed. (1987 March 25). *Opelousas Daily World.*

Boyatzis, R. E. (1998). *Transforming qualitative information: Thematic analysis and code development.* Thousand Oaks, CA: SAGE publications.

Britton, H. (1969). Chronological summary of events of student demonstration at Alcee Forties High School. In A. Fairclough. *Race and democracy: the civil rights movement in Louisiana 1915-1972.* Athens: University of Georgia Press.

Butler, J. E., & Walter, J.C. (1991). *Transforming the curriculum: Ethnic studies and women's studies.* Albany: State University of New York Press.

Butler, J. S. (1974). Black educators in Louisiana: A question of survival. *Journal of Negro Education,* pp. 36-40.

Campbell, D. (2004). *Choosing democracy: A practical guide to multicultural education.* 4th ed. Boston: Allyn and Bacon.

Chemelynski, C. (1990). Controversy attends schools with all-Black, all male classes. *The Executive Director,* 12: pp. 16-18.

Clark, K. & Clark, M. (1947). Racial identification and preference in Negro children. In T.M. Newcomb and E. Hardley (Eds.). *Readings in Psychology.* New York: Henry Holt.

Clarke, J. (1919). Introduction. In Woodson, C.G., *The education of the Negro prior to 1861.* Brooklyn: A and B Books Publishers.

Controversy at high school. (1994 February 27). *Opelousas Daily World.*

Covvarrubias, A. (1999 February). L.A. schools battle racial upheavals. *The Bakersfield Californian.*

Creswell, J. (1998). *Qualitative inquiry and research design.* Thousand Oaks, CA: SAGE Publications.

Darder, A. (2002). *Reinventing Paulo Freire: A pedagogy of love.* Boulder: Westview Press.

Davis, D. (1997). The Smith-Brown incident: Black power advocates in a struggle to redirect Southern University. M.A. Thesis, Southern University, Baton Rouge.

Dubois, W.E.B. (1989). *The souls of black folk.* New York: Penguin.

Dumbuya, A.A. (2000). A study to investigate and analyze the narrative experiences of international students studying at SouthWest Border University. Doctoral Dissertation, New Mexico State University, New Mexico.

Embree, E. (1943). *Brown Americans the story of tenth of the nation.* New York: The Viking Press.

Eure, J. & Jerome, R. (1989). *Back where we belong: Selected speeches by Louis Farrakhan.* Philadelphia: PC International Press.

Fanon, F. (1968). *The wretched of the earth.* New York: Grove Press

Fairclough, A. (1995). *Race and democracy: The civil rights movement in Louisiana 1915-1972.* Athens: University of Georgia Press.

Flanagan, J.C. (1954). The black revolution in education. In J. Banks and J. Grambs, (Eds.). *Black self concept.* New York: McGraw-Hill.

Franklin, J., Honre, G., Cruse, H., Ballard, A., & Mitchell, R. (1998). Black history month: Serious truth telling or triumph in tokenism. *Journal of Blacks in Higher Education,* 18: pp. 87-92.

Freire, P. (2000). *Pedagogy of the oppressed.* New York: Continuum.

Gay, G. (2000). *Culturally responsive teaching: Theory, Research, & Practice.* New York: Teachers College Press.

Gollinick, D., & Chinn, P. (2006). *Multicultural education in a pluralistic society and exploring diversity.* 7th edition. New Jersey: Prentice Hall.

Green, R. (1991 October). African American males' education or incarceration. Paper presented at Kellogg foundation national conference in Battle Creek, Michigan.

Hassan-El, K. (1999). *The Willie Lynch letter and the making of a slave.* Chicago, IL: Lushena Books.

Heard, D. (1990). How do teachers identify multicultural and cross cultural pedagogical phenomena in and out of arts classrooms? *Educational Review,* 42, pp. 303-318.

Hilliard, A.G. (1978). Anatomy and dynamics of oppression. Speech delivered at the national conference on human relations in education. Minneapolis, MN.

Howard, G. (2006). *We can't teach what we don't know: White teachers in multiracial schools.* New York: Teachers College Press.

Karenga, M. R. (2002). *Introduction to black studies.* Los Angeles: University of Sankore Press.

Keto, C.T. (1990). *African centered perspective of history.* Blackwood, NJ: C.A. Associates.

Kincheloe, J. & Steinberg, S. (1997). *Changing multiculturalism.* Buckingham, PA: Open University Press.

Kozol, J. (1991). *Savage inequalities: Children in America's schools.* New York: Harper Collins.

Kula, D. (1969). Protest in black and white. *National Association of Secondary School Principals Bulletin* 54: pp.72-85.

Lee, C.D. (1992). Profile of an independent black institution: African centered education at work. *Journal of Negro Education,* 61(2): pp. 160-177.

Lefkowitz, M. (1996). The Afrocentric interpretation of western history: Lefkowitz replies to Bernal. *Journal of Blacks in Higher Education,* Summer: 88-91.

Levine, A., & Cureton, J.S. (1998). *When hope and fear collide: A portrait of today's college students.* San Francisco: Jossey-Bass.

Loewen, J. (1995). *Lies my teacher told me.* New York: Touchstone.

Macedo, Donald. (2000). Introduction. In Freire, P., *Pedagogy of the oppressed.* New York: Continuum.

Marshall, C. A., & Rossman, G.B. (1985). *Designing qualitative research* (2nd ed.). Thousand Oaks, CA: SAGE Publications.

Marshall, P. (2002). *Cultural diversity in our schools.* Belmont, CA: Wadsworth Publishing.

McLaren, P.(2003). *Life in schools: An introduction to critical pedagogy in the foundations of education.* Boston: Allyn and Bacon.

Miles, M. & Huberman, A. M. (1994). *Qualitative data analysis* (2nd ed.). Thousand Oaks, CA: SAGE Publications.

Morning Advocate. (1985 September 14). Baton Rouge, La.

Moore, R. (1988). *Whistling in the wind: An autobiography of Rev. A.J. McKnight.* Lafayette, LA: Southwest Development Foundation.

Muhammad, E. (1965). *Message to the black man in America.* Chicago: Final Call.

Murray, H.T. (1978). The struggle for civil rights in New Orleans in 1960: Reflections and recollections. *Journal of Ethnic Studies* 6: pp. 25-41.

Nieto, S. (2004). *Affirming diversity: The socio-political context of multicultural education.* 4th ed. New York: Longman.

Nobles, W. (1986). *African psychology.* Oakland: Black Family Institute.

Pallas, A.M., Natriello, G., & McDill, E.L. (1989). The changing nature of the disadvantaged population: Current dimensions and future trends. *Educational Researcher* 18: pp.16-22.

Patton, Q.M. (1990). *Qualitative evaluation and research methods.* Thousand Oaks, CA: SAGE Publications.

Personnel flap sparks school board debate. (1995 August 18). *Baton Rouge Advocate.*

Pinar, W. (2004). What is curriculum theory? New Jersey: Lawrence Erlbaum Associates.

Plaisance coach among group arrests. (1987 March 27). *Opelousas Daily World.*

Principal fired. (1995 August 11). *Opelousas Daily World.*

Proposal to scuttle Afrocentric curricula sparks protest (1997 January 15). *Education Week.*

Protesters enter office arrested. (1987 March 27). *Opelousas Daily World.*

Rally to protest school sites. (1987 March 23). *Opelousas Daily World.*

Rhoads, R. (1998a). *Student activism in an age of cultural diversity.* Baltimore and London: John Hopkins University Press.

Rhoads, R. (1998b). Student protest and multicultural reform: Making sense of campus unrest in the 1990s. *Journal of Higher Education.* Nov-Dec.

Richards, D. (1991). *Let the circle be unbroken.* Trenton, NJ: Africa World Press.

Rideau, K. (1994 March 31). Another view on north central. *Opelousas Daily World.*

Schlesinger, A. (1991). The disuniting of America. *American Educator.* Vol. 15 No.3, pp. 14, 21-23.

School plans apology for speaker. (1994 February 27). *Opelousas Daily World.*

School troubles: Parents want to oust principal, 2 teachers. (1994 March 31). *Opelousas Daily World.*

Seidman, I. (1998). *Interviewing as qualitative research: A guide for researcher in education and social services.* New York: Teachers College Press.

Sesay, A. (1996). Black history month: Its origin and significance in our multicultural society. *Journal of Negro History* XLVII (3): pp. 140-150.

Site vote protested. (1987 March 24). *Opelousas Daily World.*

Stovall, D. (2005). Critical race theory as educational protest. In Watkins, W., *Black protest thought and education.* Oxford: Peter Lang Publishers.

Teacher attacked by student. (1994 March 22). *Opelousas Daily World*

Teacher says move racially motivated. (1999 July 30). *Baton Rouge Advocate.*

Teachers stage sickout. (1987 March 26). *Opelousas Daily World.*

Teacher transfer. (1995 August 24). *Opelousas Daily World.*

Vann, K. & Kunjufu, J. (1993). The importance of an Afrocentric, multicultural curriculum. *Phi Delta Kappan:* pp. 490-491.

Watkins, W. (2001). *The White architects of Black education: Ideology and power in America 1865-1954.* New York: Teachers College Press.

Watkins, W. (2005). *Black protest thought and education.* Oxford: Peter Lang Publishers.

Wetsby, R., & Braugnart, R. (1970). Activists and the history of the future. In Foster, J. and Long, D., *Protest! Student activism in America.* New York: William and Morrow.

Wilhelm, R. (1994). Exploring the practice of rhetoric gap; Current curriculum for African American history month in some Texas elementary schools. *Journal of Curriculum and Instruction* 9: pp. 217-233.

William-Evers, M. 2003). Foreword. In Bauerlein, M., Burroughs, T., Forbes, E., and Haskins, J., *Civil rights chronicle: The African American struggle for freedom.* Lincolnwood: Legacy Publishing.

Woodson, C. G. (1999). *The mis-education of the Negro* (11th ed.). Trenton, NJ: First Africa World Press.

Young, A. (1980). The historical origin and significance of black history month observation. *Negro History Bulletin* 43: pp. 6-8.
Young, J. (1971). A study of attitudes towards the relevancy of black studies in senior high schools. M.A. Thesis: Southern University.

Index